Luke Paul and the Mosque

Through this story of the Rev Luke Paul, the issues involved in opening up inter-religious dialogue and learning about inter-cultural sensitivity are thoughtfully and carefully explored. It should inspire and encourage those who might be hesitant to follow his example.

Very Rev Dr Sheilagh Kesting, Ecumenical Officer, Church of Scotland.

This is a very timely venture twelve years after 9/11 building, as it does very effectively, on encounter and experience as well as history and theology. It opens up different, and in some cases quite difficult, areas for constructive reflection and consideration, doing so in a tentative and exploratory way, and making good use of analogy so that double standards are well avoided.

Professor Hugh Goddard, Director, Prince Alwaleed Bin Talal Centre for the Study of Islam in the Contemporary World, University of Edinburgh

An imaginative and enjoyable approach to inter faith relations. It is informative and reflective. Rooted as it is in real life experiences it gently leads the reader to consider contemporary issues in a way which is open, challenging and loving without being confrontational.

Although the central character is a fictional minister of the Kirk, the issues raised are ones facing all the Christian Churches and indeed all faiths. This book will be a valuable resource for Churches and other groups interested in interfaith relations, an enjoyable read and as such a contribution to harmony and understanding in our multifaith society.

Sr Isabel Smyth, Chair, Interfaith Scotland

Luke Paul and the Mosque

Finlay A. J. Macdonald

Shoving Leopard

Shoving Leopard
8 Edina Street 2 F 3
Edinburgh, EH2 5PN
United Kingdom
http://www.shovingleopard.com/

First published in 2013
Text © Finlay A J Macdonald 2013

The cover image shows part of the ceiling of Belenardiç
village mosque, Denizli province, Turkiye.

ISBN 978-1-905565-23-8

In affectionate memory of
Alison Twaddle
1950-2013
General Secretary of the Church of Scotland Guild
1998-2011

I am dedicating this book to the memory of Alison Twaddle, General Secretary of the Church of Scotland Guild from 1998 to 2011, who died earlier this year.

Readers will discover that a significant story line involves women of the Church, through the local Guild branch, initiating a friendship with women from a nearby Mosque. This, in turn, leads to a wider interaction between Minister and Imam and their two communities. Such imagination and openness absolutely reflects the Alison I knew, and with whom I worked closely for over a decade in the national offices of the Church of Scotland. She contributed positively to the Kirk's Interfaith Forum, a body which encourages interfaith cooperation by church agencies wherever appropriate and possible. A good example is the manner in which the Guild, under Alison's leadership, helped establish the Interfaith Group on Domestic Abuse which works, with input from Scottish Women's Aid, to support faith communities in addressing this issue and raising its profile.

More generally, I hope that the part played by the women in connecting Church and Mosque, may serve to illustrate the vital, though often unsung, role played by women of faith, such as Alison, in helping to shape just and inclusive societies and a world more at ease with itself.

FAJM

Introduction

Some who read this book may also have read my last book, *Luke Paul* (Shoving Leopard, Edinburgh, 2012). This offered a fictionalised take on the gay clergy debate within the Church of Scotland as the Reverend Luke Paul and his congregation engage with the issues. The name links the generally inclusive evangelist with the sometimes dogmatic apostle and reflects my view that healthy ministerial formation draws on both.

Another neuralgic issue for the Church concerns interfaith relations. From their Lord Christians are given a clear mandate for mission. They are also called to love their neighbours as themselves remembering that, according to the famous parable of the Good Samaritan, the true neighbour can belong to a different tribe. In 1993 the General Assembly of the Church of Scotland accepted a major report entitled *Mission and Evangelism in a Multi-Faith Society.* This has underpinned much of the interfaith work of recent years. However, in 2012 the Assembly instructed a policy review in this area and called for a 'substantial report' to be presented in 2014. This will address 'all aspects of inter-faith work, with particular reference to the place and practice of Christian mission.'

Luke Paul and the Mosque locates this debate within the setting of a typical Church of Scotland parish. I have stuck with the character of Luke Paul, and here we find him reflecting on his own interfaith encounters and encouraging his congregation to share the journey with him. Written from the perspective of a Church of Scotland minister and against the background of real events and experiences, the story also involves an imagining of possibilities for developing genuine interfaith dialogue and friendship. While, as the title implies, a significant story-line involves a developing Christian-Muslim friendship, other faith communities also feature in the narrative.

The 1993 General Assembly report, referred to above, quoted from a document known as the *San Antonio Declaration* of the World Council of Churches. It is a text which has guided my thinking in this area since I first came across it all those years ago.

> *(As Christians) We cannot point to any other way of salvation than Jesus Christ; at the same time we cannot set limits to the saving power of God.*

The *Declaration* dates from 1989, twelve years before 9/11, since when further work has been undertaken by the World Council of Churches on this theme. In particular a 2006 document entitled *Religious Plurality and Christian Self-Understanding* perfectly encapsulates the thinking which seeks expression in this book:

> *The religious traditions of humankind, in their great diversity, are 'journeys' or 'pilgrimages' towards human fulfilment in search for the truth about our existence. Even though we may be 'strangers' to each other, there are moments in which our paths intersect that call for 'religious hospitality.' Both our personal experiences today and historical moments in the past witness to the*

fact that such hospitality is possible and does take place in small ways. Extending such hospitality is dependent on a theology that is hospitable to the 'other'.

I gratefully acknowledge the support of those who have been kind enough to read the original script of this book, in whole or in part, and offer suggestions which have undoubtedly improved that original. These include Sister Isabel Smyth, Chair of the Board of Interfaith Scotland and formerly Lecturer in the Centre for Interfaith Studies at Glasgow University; Iain Stewart, Secretary of the Edinburgh Interfaith Association and previously Interfaith Officer of the Church of Scotland; the Very Rev Dr John Miller, a former Moderator of the General Assembly; the Very Rev Dr Sheilagh Kesting, Church of Scotland Ecumenical Officer and a former Moderator of the General Assembly; Bailie Fariha Thomas of Glasgow City Council; Farkhanda Chaudry, Corporate Equality Officer, East Renfrewshire Council and Senior Fellow, Equality and Community Affairs, at the Curzon Institute; and Professor Hugh Goddard, Director of the University of Edinburgh's Prince Alwaleed Bin Talal Centre for the Study of Islam in the Contemporary World.

I also wish to place on record my gratitude to Dr Mona Siddiqui, Professor of Islamic and Interreligious Studies in the University of Edinburgh, with whom I had a most helpful conversation at the commencement of this project. In 2010 Professor Siddiqui became the first Muslim to address the General Assembly.

In addition I am grateful to David Fergusson, Professor of Divinity in the University of Edinburgh, for drawing my attention to the article, referred to in Chapter 15, by

Joshua Ralston of Union Presbyterian Seminary, Richmond, Virginia.

I also record my thanks to Janet de Vigne of Shoving Leopard Publishing for her encouragement and support.

Luke Paul and the Mosque is not an academic or scholarly work. There are no footnotes, index or extended bibliography. However, for the benefit of those who might which to explore further I draw attention to three books which, as a Christian seeking to learn more about Islam, I have found particularly helpful. These are *How to Read the Qur'an* by Mona Siddiqui (W.W Norton & Co, 2007), *A New Introduction to Islam, Second Edition* by Daniel W. Brown (Wiley-Blackwell, 2009) and *Allah, a Christian Response* by Miroslav Volf (Harper One 2011).

Quotations from the *Qur'an* are taken from the Pickthall English translation.

With the exception of obviously identifiable individuals the principal characters are my own creation. Any resemblance to real people whose names happen to feature is entirely coincidental. Also, it will be a matter of real regret if Luke's musing on the beliefs and practices of different religions gives cause for offence. That could not be further from my purpose in a book which is born of interest and respect.

Finlay A. J. Macdonald
Scottish Interfaith Week, 2013

1

Settling back into every day church life was not as easy as the Reverend Luke Paul had anticipated.

His ministry of nearly forty years, in three parishes, had been largely uncontroversial –unadventurous even - though, looking back, perhaps it had been a bit *avant-garde* to push for women elders in the early 1970s in his first charge – the village of Glenburn, near Inverness. In St Fillan's, Dundee in the late 80s he had fostered an ecumenical link with a Roman Catholic order of nuns who were resident within the community. That might have attracted criticism in more sectarianly sensitive parts of Scotland but it occasioned little controversy on the banks of the Tay.

After twenty years in Dundee Luke moved to what he anticipated would be his final charge. This was the large village/small town of Capelaw to the south of Edinburgh, from where he was due to retire within the next few years. Here he had continued his ecumenical interests and, indeed expanded these through a growing interest in interfaith dialogue. However, any ripples of controversy this created paled into insignificance when Luke found himself embroiled in the most divisive issue which he had faced in all his years as a minister – the question of whether persons in same-sex relationships should be ordained as ministers of the Church of Scotland.

The General Assembly of 2009 had appointed a Special Commission to look at this question in depth, including a large scale canvassing of opinion across the Church. The consultation took the form of a series of questions which kirk sessions and presbyteries were to debate and then answer individually and privately. This process was particularly sensitive at congregational level. It was not the sort of subject which normally found its way on to a kirk session's agenda. There was disagreement and sometimes this was of the kind which damaged relationships. In addition, the topic was one on which most ministers preferred to keep their opinions to themselves, in the interests of preserving good pastoral relations. So when, in the autumn of 2010, the material duly arrived from head office Luke groaned to his wife, Joyce:

"Why could this not have waited until I had retired?"

Joyce's practical reply was along the lines that Luke would not be the only minister expressing such sentiments, but he would just have to get on with it. For good measure she added that in her own career as a teacher she had had to deal with endless forms and questionnaires from the Education Department which, in her humble opinion, distracted from her real job of teaching children.

The ensuing months were certainly stressful and perhaps Luke brought some of this upon himself. His own view of the matter was liberal and progressive. He was persuaded by the argument that a person's sexuality was given and not chosen. He had welcomed the creation of civil partnerships which allowed gay people to enter into a solemn and faithful commitment and, provided gay ministers chose fidelity over promiscuity, he saw no real problem. Of course there were those within the congregation who took a different view and some of these 'lifted their lines' (resigned their membership), particularly after Luke decided to preach sympathetically on the subject one Sunday. However, this loss was compensated for by a number of people expressing appreciation of what he had said, including people who were themselves gay or who had gay sons or daughters. One of these was Ailsa, a young woman who helped run the church youth club. Encouraged by Luke's gay-friendly approach she asked if he would bless a civil partnership she was entering into with another young woman, Liz. Luke agreed and this created more difficulty in the parish, with threats of resignation from elders and a complaint by a ministerial colleague to the presbytery. That complaint came to nothing in the end, but Luke stood his ground. Then when the matter came before the General Assembly in May 2011 he spoke in the debate in favour of allowing openly gay individuals to become ministers. His speech was broadcast on the BBC's Assembly coverage and that didn't go down well in some quarters.

Luke's stance also created some tension within his own family. His son, Richard, a chartered accountant, was a church treasurer in Fife and took a different view from his father. Richard's argument was that the Bible contained passages which clearly condemned homosexual activity and people couldn't just pick and choose which bits of the Bible they liked. On a more day to day level Richard was also concerned about loss of members and revenue from his own congregation, as a consequence of the Church's willingness even to discuss the matter. By contrast Luke's daughter, Anne, who had followed her mother into teaching, thoroughly approved of her father's stance and wondered what all the 'stushie' was about. Joyce, as ever, was loyal to her husband and admired him for standing up to those whose disagreement verged on the intemperate.

So the parish year 2010-2011 had been somewhat fraught and, as Luke travelled home from the General Assembly in May 2011, after contributing to the debate and seeing the Assembly preferring an enabling motion over a blocking one, he was pleased but also looking forward to putting the past year behind him. It will be good, he thought, to settle back to the everyday routine tasks of a parish minister, free of divisive controversy and argument.

The reality, though, was rather different as, somewhat to his surprise, Luke discovered that he had rather enjoyed the controversy – the notoriety even! He was quite proud of the fact that, in the twilight of his ministry, he had faced a possible disciplinary process for blessing a civil partnership. Son Richard had been appalled but daughter Anne was really quite proud of her old dad — and Joyce? She was furious that a fellow minister would dare to suggest her diligent and decent husband had acted in a way that might merit discipline. Luke put that down as supportive too.

While the 2011 General Assembly had set a direction of travel towards the possibility of the Church accepting openly gay ministers it had also set up a Theological Commission to work out the practical implications of this. This new Commission would report in 2013. As a minister's turn to attend the Assembly came round every four years Luke would not be going. He had had his say in 2011 and that was fine.

The summer months are something of a 'close season' in parish life. Church organisations are in recess, schools are on holiday, few meetings are held, many people are away from home. Come late August, though, the pace quickens as schools return and soon everything springs into life as the range of activities for young and old resumes from Brownies to Friendship Club. Luke and Joyce took their holiday in Italy, based in Sorrento but generally exploring the Bay of Naples. They even made it to the top of Vesuvius. Luke enjoyed telling people that, though Joyce, with an annoying attention to detail, always insisted on adding that there was a coach park two hundred feet below the summit. As he peered into the crater Luke wondered if the Kirk might yet erupt over the question of gay ministers as it had 'disrupted' in 1843 over issues of the day which were equally contentious. Certainly over the summer and into the autumn there were reports of ministers and congregations leaving the Church or threatening to do so. Church officials pointed out that a final decision would not be taken before 2013, but those intent on going replied that the direction of travel was already clear and that, in conscience, they could no longer remain.

Against these continuing rumblings Luke preached Sunday by Sunday, baptised babies, married brides and grooms, conducted funeral services in crematoria and at gravesides, visited the sick at home and hospital, presided at session meetings, attended presbytery meetings – all of which he found fulfilling. Yet he missed the excitement of the previous year's lively discussions and the engagement with a new questioning of accepted ways of thinking. It had been particularly good to focus on issues of discrimination and justice which were so close to home. People had been challenged to study the Bible, to see what it said and to consider how words, first written down centuries ago, were to be interpreted and applied in the very different setting of twenty-first century Scotland. The arguments over Ailsa and Liz's civil partnership had been painful at the time but is it not the case, thought Luke, that there is no gain without pain? As he looked out from the pulpit on Sundays it seemed that something had changed within the congregational dynamic. They no longer avoided difficult questions such as how human sexuality seeks different forms of expression; rather they had engaged with the issues and were the better for it – more mature, more honest. Perhaps, Luke reflected, we should continue along this path and explore other contentious matters we often prefer to avoid.

One evening he articulated this thought to Joyce as they shared their evening meal –on this occasion a meal unusually not interrupted by the telephone.

"Go for it," was her response. "I've sensed that you've been a bit restless and looking for a new challenge. Do you have something in mind?"

"I'm not sure," answered Luke "but no doubt something will turn up which fits the bill."

2

And it did.

The very next morning Luke opened his *Scotsman* newspaper. There was a story about an Aberdeen church which was allowing its hall to be used for worship by a local Hindu community which had no premises of its own. This, Luke noted, was not reported as a good news story about interfaith friendship offering a beacon of hope in a divided world. Rather, the coverage focussed on a motion which had been lodged with the local presbytery seeking action to ban the use of church premises for this purpose. In particular the motion referred to 'sacrificial worship offered to false deities in contravention of the first and second commandments.' In reply the minister of the congregation stated: 'They (the Hindus) are lovely people. They are part of our local community and they are welcome. We don't have any problem with it at all.' The *Scotsman* report went on to state that, after a debate held in private, the banning motion was narrowly defeated.

It troubled Luke that religion seemed to lie at the root of so many divisions, often adding a particularly toxic dimension of its own. It had distressed him that the vicious 1990s conflict following the breakup of the former Yugoslavia involved Catholic Croatia, Orthodox Serbia and Muslim Bosnia; yet did not protestations of peace and love lie at the heart of both Christianity and lslam? Indeed, it was often said that the very term 'Islam' reflected the Arabic word for 'peace' – *Salaam*. One might reasonably have hoped that religious teaching could mitigate ethnic and political tensions but, on the contrary, it appeared only to feed and exacerbate them.

Before that, and closer to home, had been the 'troubles' in Northern Ireland between Unionist/Protestant and Republican/Catholic. The religious dimension of that prolonged conflict deeply offended Luke. Indeed, at one point it led him seriously to contemplate giving up his studies for the ministry. Would people think that as a presbyterian minister he identified with the ranting flowing from the mouths of men in bowler hats and orange sashes? Indeed he sometimes wondered whether it was entirely a coincidence that the decades marked by the Irish troubles had seen such a decline in both protestant and catholic church attendance in mainland Britain. Who could blame ordinary, decent people for thinking: if that's Christianity it's not for me?

Of course, and by way of redressing the balance, Luke acknowledged that these same years had seen an increase in ecumenical co-operation amongst Christians of different denominations, often uniting in the pursuit of reconciliation. Indeed it was remarked (and probably accurately) that at the height of the Irish troubles the 'real' Christians on both sides of the sectarian and political divide had never been closer. But such closeness was not the stuff of which headlines were made. Inevitably it was conflict rather than co-operation which made the news.

It was also the case that Scotland had its own sectarian tale to tell of how the predominant protestant churches had been less than welcoming to impoverished Irish immigrants (and their descendants) fleeing famine in the nineteenth century.

Growing up in Glasgow in the 1950s Luke had been aware from an early age of the different cultures gathered round Church and Chapel, Rangers and Celtic. Depressingly, five decades later, as the twentieth century yielded to the twenty-first, it was still necessary for the Scottish Government to place anti-sectarian policies high on its agenda.

But things had moved on - within the churches at least. Every January most denominations observed a Week of Prayer for Christian Unity, with Christians from the various traditions – Presbyterian, Catholic, Baptist, Episcopal, Methodist, Quaker – sharing in services, with opportunity afterwards for hospitality and conversation. In most areas of the country local clergy from across the denominational spread would meet monthly to drink coffee, share stories, seek advice and generally enjoy one another's company. In Capelaw Luke belonged to just such a group and could not but contrast it with the 'fraternal' of male Church of Scotland ministers to which he belonged at the start of his ministry, nearly forty years earlier. And, while in retrospective mode, Luke also recalled being present in the momentous General Assembly of 1975 when, for the first time since the Reformation of 1560, a Roman Catholic visitor addressed the Assembly. It was also Luke's first Assembly as an ordained minister, so it made an impression on these grounds alone. But the real history was made when Archbishop Thomas Winning was invited to speak. No doubt some regarded this as a betrayal, but most saw it as a sign of hope for the future. The archbishop began by asking "what do brothers say to one another after years – and in our case centuries – of silence? Surely, they ask for forgiveness". He concluded by expressing a commitment to work with the Church of Scotland and other Christian Churches towards unity. After thanking the Archbishop the Moderator, Dr James Matheson, invited the Assembly to stand and say the doxology together: *Glory be to the Father and to the Son and to the Holy Ghost; as it was in the beginning, is now and shall be evermore, Amen.*" Over the ensuing years of his ministry Luke was to become a strong supporter of ecumenism. Looking back he wondered if the seed of that enthusiasm had been sown at that memorable first General Assembly.

In more recent years that ecumenical drive had expanded to encompass interfaith relations. In September of 2001 Luke had attended a special service in St Giles' Cathedral to reflect on the 9/11 attack on the United States and to pray for all directly affected by that atrocity. He took his seat and was shortly joined by a young and tearful American woman. After pausing for silent prayer she perused the Order of Service sheet, then froze and became more visibly upset.

"Are you all right?" Luke inquired.

"Not really," she replied. "I can't believe they've got a reading from the *Qur'an* in the service."

And indeed they did, along with readings from the Jewish Scriptures/Old Testament and the New Testament. And so the service proceeded. When it was over the young woman, who it turned out was from New York, turned to Luke and said:

"I'm sorry about my outburst earlier. I never knew there was stuff like that in the *Qur'an*. It was beautiful. It reminded me of that bit in Romans where St Paul talks of overcoming evil with good and the passage in the Sermon on the Mount where Jesus said we are to love our enemies. That's certainly pretty hard at a time like this," she added.

These are the verses:

> *O mankind! Lo! We have created you male and female, and have made you nations and tribes that ye may know one another. Lo! the noblest of you, in the sight of Allah, is the best in conduct. Lo! Allah is Knower, Aware. (Q49:13)*

> *The good deed and the evil deed are not alike. Repel the evil deed with one which is better, then lo! he, between whom and thee there was enmity (will become) as though he was a bosom friend.*

> *But none is granted it save those who are steadfast, and none is granted it save the owner of great happiness. (Q 41:34-35)*

The young woman and Luke chatted as they left the Cathedral. She had just arrived in Edinburgh as an exchange student from the States. She had been in touch with her family in New York who were, mercifully, fine but they had told her of neighbours and acquaintances who had been less fortunate. Again she apologised for her initial outburst but went on to explain that she didn't know any Muslims and had grown up thinking they were some kind of enemy.

"After what has just happened," she added "a lot of my fellow citizens will feel confirmed in that view. That's what my heart feels but my head tells me that we need to get beyond that mind-set."

They never met again but the encounter remained with Luke as a vivid memory for years to come.

What he didn't share with the young American woman was that, while surprising to her, the gesture of interfaith respect – by including a reading from the *Qur'an* – was not a first for St Giles'. Ten years earlier, in October 1991, a service in memory of victims of the first Gulf War had been held there and was attended by Muslims. Twenty minutes into the service a Muslim time of prayer arrived. The service was paused, the *Adhan* call to prayer was made from the Cathedral pulpit and the Muslim members of the congregation made their prayers next to the Holy Table. The prayers completed, the service resumed and continued to its conclusion.

Luke had thought of sharing this story with his new American friend but, sensitive to her fragility and pain, decided not to. However, later that day, on the bus back to Capelaw, as he reflected on the encounter he found himself thinking of a recent visit to his old 'bishop', Edward Bryan, then in his nineties. Luke had cut his ministerial teeth as assistant to Edward in a busy Glasgow inner-city parish and they had kept in touch over the years. Edward was now resident in a Church of Scotland 'eventide' home in Edinburgh and on the occasion of this visit Luke had been somewhat taken aback to find the old boy reading the *Qur'an*.

"That's different!" Luke observed.

"Well, at my age," Edward replied, with a decided twinkle in his eye, "time's getting on and I thought it might be useful to get a second opinion! There's a lot of interesting stuff in here, some of it quite like the Bible."

Ninety years young, marvelled Luke. If I make it to my nineties I hope I'm half as sharp.

3

Like many Luke had seen 9/11 as a deeply troubling pointer to the animosity which had become a feature of interpersonal and international relations – east and west, rich and poor, black and white, Asian and European, Christian and Muslim, Jew and Arab, haves and have-nots – the list was endless. It was inevitable that the Americans would go after those behind the atrocity, so it was no great surprise when the bombardment of *Al-Qaeda* redoubts in Afghanistan began in the autumn of 2001. Whether anyone thought that after more than a decade American and NATO troops would still be there was another matter. Then there was the invasion of Iraq a year and a bit later, despite the fact that Iraq had had no involvement in 9/11. Luke had marched against that war and had been particularly incensed when the American President had used the word 'crusade' in the general context of fighting a 'war on terror'. Luke was not alone in finding this objectionable and was particularly pleased when church leaders around the world, including in the United States, had dissociated themselves from such language. For all that, the sheer destructive force of the 'shock and awe' made it increasingly difficult to maintain the line that the bombing of Baghdad was not a declaration of war by a Christian west against a Muslim Middle East.

Luke had been encouraged therefore when, in response to 9/11, Scotland's church leaders had invited all Scotland's faith communities to send a representative to a gathering at Scottish Churches' House, Dunblane. The invitation was accepted and together the faith leaders (as they came to be known) met, talked, listened, told stories, shared food, prayed each in their own way and lastly, but by no means least, agreed to keep meeting. This they did over the coming years in churches, mosques, synagogues, mandirs and temples– Baha'i, Buddhist, Christian, Hindu, Jew, Muslim and Sikh – people of different traditions who had in common that they were all people of faith and all Scottish.

It was around this time that Luke received an invitation which he just couldn't refuse. For a number of years he had been a member of the Church's Ecumenical Relations Committee and in early 2002 he had written an article in *Ministers' Forum*. This journal provided a platform for ministers to exchange ideas on current issues, safe in the knowledge that these would be read only by fellow ministers. Luke's article, written in the aftermath of 9/11, was a plea for the Church of Scotland to move beyond the mere ecumenical zone of engaging with other Christian denominations. Now was the time, he argued, to make contacts with adherents of other faiths living within our communities. Just as once upon a time, he suggested, the easy relationships which now existed between priest and minister would have been unimaginable, so a time would come when today's complete lack of contact between minister and imam or rabbi or local Sikh leader would be unimaginable. Luke's article had attracted both favourable and negative comment. Some agreed that the example set by the religious leaders, who now met regularly together, should be followed at local level. Others argued that, as evangelism was central to Christian teaching, the only legitimate reason for engaging with people of other faiths was in order to convert them to the one true faith, namely Christianity.

Luke's article had particularly attracted the notice of those who were assembling a small delegation to accompany the Moderator at an ecumenical consultation being held in Beirut and hosted by the National Evangelical Synod of Syria and Lebanon. Also attending the event would be representatives of the United Reformed Church and the Presbyterian Church in Ireland. Once the conference was over Luke would accompany the Moderator and his party on a visit to neighbouring Syria. The dates were free in Luke's diary – or so far ahead as to be easily cleared – so after discussing it with his wife Joyce and his Session Clerk, Brian MacFarlane, he accepted the invitation. Apart from participating in an organised pilgrimage to the Holy Land Luke had never been to the Middle East. He realised that this would be a very different experience, and so it was to turn out.

The consultation was due to be held at a centre in the hills above Beirut but a heavy snowfall made that impossible, so it was quickly re-arranged for the Near East School of Theology in Beirut itself. The principal theme was 'Identity' with each participating church focussing on its own identity within its own context and then reflecting together on similarities and differences. Most marked, inevitably, was the very different setting in which the three UK denominations worked within an officially Christian country, compared with the context of the National Evangelical Synod of Syria and Lebanon within a predominantly Islamic culture. The marginal nature of that church was further emphasised by its minority place within Syria's Christian communities, which were predominately

Orthodox. This marginalisation was even further accentuated by the fact that the Orthodox Christians maintained a powerful claim to be indigenous to Syria. After all was Saul of Tarsus not converted on the road to Damascus? By contrast the Evangelical churches were the product of western missionary movements whose ecclesiastical patterns were still apparent in worship and government. Luke had been amazed when, a couple of days before the consultation, he had visited a church in southern Lebanon and, on picking up a music hymn book, had spotted a number of familiar Scottish psalm tunes. Even more astonishing was to find the music written out from right to left, following the pattern of the Arabic words. He was not surprised, therefore, that an issue which came up during the conference was the need to stress local credentials by making greater use of indigenous middle-eastern music in worship.

Another illustration of the marginalising of Evangelical Christians was a prohibition on holding civic or political office. Such office was open only to Orthodox Christians and Muslims. Luke could not but contrast this with his own position as a parish minister of the Church of Scotland. While, undeniably fewer people went to Church than when he had started out four decades earlier, the fact remained that the parish minister retained a certain social standing and recognition within the community. Also, the Church of Scotland itself was acknowledged as a national church, with its ministers available to any who sought their services and not just to paid-up members of the congregation. By contrast, being a member of an Evangelical church in Lebanon or Syria, he thought, must be a bit like being a Muslim or a Hindu in Scotland – part of a tiny minority, often viewed with suspicion and even distrust by the majority.

The Beirut consultation was held in late February 2003, when the prospect of an American led invasion of Iraq was looking more and more likely. Aircraft carriers and frigates were assembling in the Gulf, troop movements were under way – all the bellicose signals were there and this was making things even harder for the Evangelical Christian community. Luke had a long conversation with a recently ordained minister who served two congregations. One was in eastern Syria near to the border with Iraq while the other was just across the border in Iraq itself. Their predominately Muslim neighbours viewed him and his church members with increasing suspicion, making a connection between what they perceived as a westward looking denomination and the threatened invasion by what they regarded as western Christians. This was a classic setting, the young minister feared, for an outbreak of ethnic cleansing and already a number of families had moved away. Indeed he confessed to some anxiety about being at the conference and leaving his wife and children at home. Luke thought of the Islamophobia which back home was not always latent and realised there was a symmetry here. He also recognised that from his stance as a member of a social, religious and ethnic majority it was very difficult to imagine the menace of living as a member of a threatened minority.

Following the conference the Church of Scotland delegation, led by the Moderator, travelled on to Syria where a number of visits had been arranged to both Christian and Muslim communities. The hovering war clouds had clearly moved the local church organisers to create opportunities for Christian-Muslim solidarity in face of so much fear and distrust.

The first visit was to the city of Aleppo, a place whose very name had fascinated Luke since, as a school-boy he had read Shakespeare's *Macbeth*. In an early scene the three witches appear and one has the lines:

A sailor's wife had chestnuts in her lap,
And munched, and munched, and munched. "Give me," quoth I.
"Aroint thee, witch!" the rump-fed runnion cries.
Her husband's to Aleppo gone, master o' th' Tiger;
But in a sieve I'll thither sail,
And like a rat without a tail,
I'll do, I'll do, and I'll do.

Now, very many years later, Aleppo was not to disappoint in the fascination stakes. For example, one thing Luke did not expect to find there was a presbyterian church with a kirk session – just like home, he thought with a smile. The congregation was part of the Evangelical Synod and a very pleasant evening was spent by the Church of Scotland group as guests of the kirk session over a meal in a local restaurant.

The next fascinating thing occurred on a visit to Aleppo's famous *Souk* – the centuries old market with stall after stall of foods and spices, clothes and all manner of goods – the air fragrant with 'all the perfumes of Arabia' (to quote *Macbeth* again) and filled by the sounds of haggling, interspersed with the call to prayer from the minaret of the Great Mosque. The Scottish group stopped to admire some fine Persian carpets. When the stall holder heard their conversation he interrupted:

"English?"

"No, Scottish," replied the Moderator.

"Ah, Scottish," responded the stall holder. "Fit like?"

Well, talk about step back in amazement!

"Where did you learn that?" asked the Moderator.

The answer was that this Syrian seller of carpets had spent a year studying at Aberdeen University in the 1970s.

The third fascinating encounter was at a deeper and more serious level altogether. This was a meeting between the Moderator and the Great Mufti of Aleppo, Sheik Ahmed Badr-Din Hassoun. The Mufti, the highest Islamic authority in the city, was warm in his welcome and engaging in his conversation, so much so that the meeting significantly overran its scheduled time. Reference was made to Abraham, the common ancestor of Christians, Muslims and Jews who are all referred to in the *Qur'an* as 'people of the book'. Abraham had two sons – Isaac, born to his wife Sarah, and Ishmael, born previously to Sarah's Egyptian slave-girl Hagar, when Sarah could not conceive. As the boys grew Sarah became resentful and pressed Abraham to banish Hagar and Ishmael; so they were forced out into the wilderness. But there God cared for them. Tradition has it that Jews and Christians are spiritual descendants of Abraham through Isaac while the Arab/Muslim line comes down through Ishmael. The Mufti even made a joke about it.

"Your mother was the blonde," he quipped to the Moderator; "mine was the brunette".

But then he put forward an altogether fascinating and thought-provoking comment. The Moderator had suggested a certain symmetry, with Muslims a minority within a predominately Christian culture in Scotland, while Christians found themselves a minority within a predominately Muslim Syria. The Mufti resisted the argument insisting that Muslims were also Christians since the *Qur'an* attaches great importance to Jesus Christ as a significant prophet and teacher.

There's another fascinating Aleppo moment, mused Luke, as he tried to absorb what the Mufti was saying. Thinking back to his undergraduate Logic course he tried to construct a syllogism in his head: All Muslims are Christians; all Christians worship God through Jesus Christ; therefore all Muslims . . . He decided not to share the thought lest it get lost in translation. At the conclusion of the meeting the Moderator was invited to sign the Mufti's Visitors' Book. Luke noticed that the previous signature was that of the Aga Khan.

From Aleppo the party travelled to Damascus and shared a little joke about being in the steps of St Paul on the road to Damascus. The capital also brought another significant encounter when the Moderator was asked to convey a Christian greeting to the large congregation gathered for Friday prayers in the Abu Nour Mosque. There the Grand Mufti of Syria, Sheik Ahmed Kuftaro welcomed the Church of Scotland party as 'cousins in faith' and followers of his 'Uncle Jesus Christ'. A nice family image, felt Luke, and in line with the Grand Mufti's track record on inter-faith relations. He had read that Sheik Kuftaro had once remarked: 'If a Muslim does not acknowledge Jesus then his Islam is for naught'. The Moderator, choosing his words carefully, responded warmly to the welcome and offered some thoughts on the Christian season of Lent which the Church was then observing. The season is one, he observed, when Christians remember that Jesus was tempted by the devil and reflect on how evil forces still stalk our world. Then, noting that he was speaking not far from the Street called Straight where St Paul had stayed after his conversion, he quoted the apostle. In his letter to the church in Rome Paul had urged Christians not to be overcome by evil but to overcome evil with good. These were deeply worrying times in the Middle-East and wider world, he continued, but if war was coming in neighbouring Iraq it should not be seen as a war between Christians and Muslims. Many church leaders in the west had spoken against such a war. As 'people of the book', with a shared heritage of faith going back to Abraham, Christians and Muslims should together seek out the good paths of peace and justice.

"What an altogether amazing experience." This was Luke to Joyce when he arrived back home in Capelaw. "I've got enough material for a year's sermons and I'll probably bore you to death over the coming weeks with tales from Lebanon and Syria."

"But seriously," he added, "I never thought I would see a Church of Scotland minister giving a Christian greeting in a mosque and certainly not a mosque in Damascus. But if it can be done in Syria, why not in Scotland?"

Note: *The events recounted in this chapter occurred in February and March 2003, shortly before the invasion of Iraq. Nine years later, in 2012, the ancient Souk in Aleppo was destroyed in the civil war, as was much of that city and those of its population who had not already fled. Sheik Kuftaro died in 2004 at the age of 92 and was succeeded as Grand Mufti of Syria by Sheik al-Badr Hassoun. In 2011 a twenty-two year old son of Sheik Hassoun was assassinated in an ambush on the road between Idlib and Aleppo.*

4

A two hour time difference barely registers on the jet lag scale. Nevertheless, Luke did not find it easy to settle back to life in Capelaw after such exposure to the culture of the Middle East, and at such an explosive time. Literally! Just a fortnight after his return home he woke to the news that the 'shock and awe' attack on Baghdad had begun.

He thought of Mr Kandalaft.

Mr Kandalaft was an elderly resident of a church-run home in the city of Homs. The Church of Scotland delegation had spent a day in Homs and Luke had been seated beside Mr Kandalaft at lunch. The old man, with tears in his eyes, spoke of his fears over what was coming. He explained that his daughter was married to an Iraqi accountant. They had three young children and they lived in Baghdad. Mr Kandalaft also told Luke that as a young engineer he had worked on the Hydro Electric scheme at Pitlochry and had greatly enjoyed his time in Scotland. Now Luke was safely back in Scotland – but what fate was befalling Mr Kandalaft's precious family and their neighbours?

Luke had made two decisions on his return from Syria.

One: he would read the *Qur'an*, like his old 'bishop' Edward Bryan. After visiting the old boy that day he had resolved that this was something he should do but, somehow, had never got round to. Now he would make time for what he anticipated would be an interesting project.

Two: he would give a reasonably full account of his time in Lebanon and Syria to his kirk session when they next met. He wasn't sure how the church elders would react but the Church of Scotland had paid his expenses and so, he felt, was entitled to get something back, if only at local level.

As it happened the kirk session of Capelaw Parish Church was due to meet the week after Luke's return from Syria. The agenda comprised mainly routine business — arrangements for Easter celebrations, an appeal from the Christian Aid Week organiser for volunteer collectors, the report of a committee which had been looking into an incident at a recent meeting of the youth club – referred to by senior elder Bob MacEwan (who could turn a nice phrase) as 'an affray to the effusion of blood'. As the club leaders had managed to calm things down without involving the police it was decided that no further action, beyond maintaining a watching brief, was required.

Such business having been efficiently despatched, Luke duly reported on his visit with the Moderator to Syria and Lebanon. He spoke of the Church of Scotland's historic links with the Evangelical Synod and the challenges faced by the members of that church today. As it had to Luke, it came as news to the elders that there was a presbyterian church with a kirk session in Aleppo, and they certainly enjoyed the story of the stall holder in the *souk* who had lived in Aberdeen and greeted the Moderator's party with a cheery "fit like?" Some eyebrows were raised when Luke spoke about meetings with Muslim muftis, and when he followed this with an account of the Moderator's address in the mosque the response of one elder, known for his plain speaking was:

"Would the Moderator not be better employed encouraging people to go to church here in Scotland than gadding about the world talking to Muslims?"

This was Jimmy Souter, local plumber and not a man to upset. You never knew when you might need his services – in a hurry. As ever, Jimmy was ready with what he liked to call his 'reality check'.

"I don't think that's very fair, Jimmy," interjected Maggie Russell, owner of the florist shop in the High Street. (Niceties such as addressing the chair were not always observed in Capelaw kirk session). We've just seen the Middle East going up in flames and it's less than two years since the attacks on the Twin Towers in New York. Surely at a time like this it's important that Christians and Muslims should speak to each other and try to break down the barriers."

"That's all very well," opined Peter Henderson, pal and regular golfing partner of Jimmy Souter, "but we're not the ones who put up the barriers. People come to this country from places like India and Pakistan and make no effort to integrate into our society; and how many Muslims living in Scotland would have been cheering on the attacks on New York?"

Sensing Peter was urging his anti-immigration hobby horse into a gallop Luke intervened:

"I think we should focus on the matter in hand. I'd be very happy to answer any questions on my visit to Syria and Lebanon."

"I have a question," said Brian MacFarlane, the session clerk. "What is the official position of the Church of Scotland on Christian-Muslim relations?"

"That's a good question," replied Luke.

"About ten years ago," he amplified, "the General Assembly debated a report on how Christians in Scotland should relate to the increasingly diverse society in which we now live. It was quite controversial. The report called for dialogue and attempts to break down some of the barriers while, of course, not compromising the integrity of the Christian faith. I was at the Assembly that year," continued Luke. "It was 1993, I think. Those who had prepared the report simply wanted the Assembly to welcome it as a basis for further study and to encourage interfaith conversations at local level. However, a minister, while not openly disagreeing with that, also wanted the Assembly to reaffirm the uniqueness of Christ as the only source of salvation. In effect, he wanted the Assembly to state, within the specific context of discussing this report, that all other religions are misguided and false."

"This created a problem for the convener presenting the report," Luke went on to explain.

"Clearly she didn't find this helpful, but had to choose her words carefully lest she be accused of heresy. It was apparent that she had anticipated such a move because she just happened to have to hand a statement from a nineteenth century constitutional document which affirmed Jesus Christ as Saviour and Lord but went on to say that 'it was not the position of the Church that God may not extend his grace to any beyond the pale of ordinary means, as may seem good in his sight'.

"Nowadays, to suggest something is beyond the pale has a rather negative connotation," explained Luke, "but in its time this was an enlightened recognition that human beings should not presume to limit the grace of God. In any event, the reporting convener went on to argue that you wouldn't get very far in a conversation if you started out by saying we are right and you are wrong. This was enough to sway the Assembly. The amendment was lost, though a fair number of people asked that their dissent be recorded."

"It was a good report," concluded Luke, "and knowing we were going to be talking about this tonight I re-read it the other day. One thing I particularly liked in it was a statement from a World Council of Churches meeting in San Antonio, Texas. Known as the San Antonio Declaration it states: 'We cannot point to any other way of salvation than Jesus Christ; at the same time we cannot set limits to the saving power of God.'"

"I don't know if that answers your question, Brian," said Luke with a smile, "but it's the best I can do."

"I think that's a very helpful statement."

This was Jean Thompson, a relative newcomer to Capelaw who had joined the kirk session just the previous year. Jean taught history at one of Edinburgh's famous Merchant Company schools.

"One of the things I struggle with," she continued, "is this idea that the Christians are right and everyone else is wrong. Even the Bible gives out mixed messages," she added for good measure.

"Sadly," she went on, "I'm at the stage of life where I find myself attending funerals rather more often than I would wish. Nearly always the minister reads verses from St John's Gospel which strike me as being self-contradictory. It's the bit where Jesus says: 'I am the way, the truth and the life; no-one comes to the Father but by me'. But just a few verses earlier he has said: 'In my Father's house are many mansions'.

Which is it?" she asked, rhetorically it appeared, because she continued in full flow: "Indeed I have a friend who claims to take great comfort from the many mansions idea because there are lots of people with whom she would prefer not share eternity too closely."

This created a ripple of amusement. Even the minister could not resist a smile, remarking "Wasn't there someone who announced that she had lots of friends she couldn't stand?"

Jean pressed on: "History is full of tragic examples of inability to respect difference and, even sadder is the role so often played by religion in the conflicts which ensue. Some terrible things have been done by religious people convinced that they were acting for God, and that includes Christians. Only last week one of my classes was looking at the story of Thomas Aitkenhead, an eighteen year old who was executed in Edinburgh in 1698 for making disparaging comments about Christianity and the Church. The Church could have intervened but chose not to. One of my pupils remarked: 'Just like the Taliban in Afghanistan'. Out of the mouths . . ."

"So," Jean concluded, "I'm all for affirming the teachings of Jesus Christ and acknowledging him as my Saviour and Lord, but don't ask me to believe in a God who cares only about the Christians."

"Well said, Jean!" Maggie Russell chimed in. "I don't have your background but that's an appalling story about young Thomas. Did that really happen just a few miles from here and a mere 300 years ago? I'm glad the Kirk doesn't have that much power today!"

"Well, let's not get too carried away," intervened Luke. "The sad truth is that the way some of our forebears behaved was not unlike the behaviour of those the media today like to describe as fundamentalists or extremists. Thank goodness we have moved on. But perhaps that makes it even more incumbent upon us to try to reach out a hand of friendship to those who are different from us. Certainly one thing Jesus did say unequivocally was that we should love our neighbour as ourself; and when he was asked to say what he meant by 'neighbour' he told the parable of the Good Samaritan. The punch-line of that story is that the only one who helped the injured man was someone from a different tribe – after two individuals from his own tribe had passed by on the other side."

These comments from the chair attracted a sage nodding of heads and no-one else seemed inclined to keep the conversation going. In any event it was almost half past nine; people had homes to go to and work the next morning. Brian MacFarlane, the session clerk, thanked Luke for sharing his experiences. He confessed that he had had some anxieties over Luke's safety in such a volatile area at such a fraught time and had been mightily relieved when he heard that he had arrived home in one piece. On behalf of the Session he thanked Luke for helping the elders see beyond the day to day affairs of Capelaw Parish Church and for giving them some insights into the work of the Church in another part of the world.

Brian's words prompted the traditional foot stamping which signifies presbyterian approval. Then everyone stood as Luke pronounced the benediction and closed the meeting.

5

"How did it go?" asked Joyce, when Luke returned home about 10 o'clock. "Shall I put the kettle on or was it a 'dram' meeting?"

She suspected the former, as the latter (which called for a glass of whisky) was usually signalled by a loud banging of the car door.

"A cup of tea will be fine," replied Luke. "It was a good meeting and I think folk quite enjoyed having something different to get their teeth into. Do you know old Brian was really concerned for my safety in Syria? I was quite touched when he said how relieved he was to know I was back in one piece."

"Well that makes two of us," Joyce retorted, "four if you include Anne and Richard. They were on the phone every other night to ask if I had heard from you."

Quite apart from gender, Luke and Joyce's children were very different people. Anne was rumbustious, feisty, and left-leaning. Richard was more withdrawn, though no push-over, and quite conservative in his approach to questions of politics and social issues. When they were both home at Christmas a lively argument had blown up over some item of news from Israel. Luke couldn't recall the specific incident but he did remember Anne passionately defending the Palestinian corner while Richard gently but firmly articulated the Israeli position. Over 9/11 too they had argued – Richard expressing pure outrage at the atrocity; Anne amplifying her condemnation with a critique of United States global policies as they impacted upon poorer and weaker nations. And, when the previous year Luke himself had marched against the prospect of an invasion of Iraq, Anne had joined him while Richard, though no war-monger, felt that particular gesture wasn't for him.

"So the kids were worried about their old dad," said Luke. "Well that's nice to know."

Over a cup of tea Luke outlined the discussion at the Session meeting. Joyce hadn't heard the story of Thomas Aitkenhead and was shocked that such a young and probably naïve young man could have been so appallingly treated.

"Yes," said Luke, "everyone seemed quite affected when Jean told that story."

"So what's on tomorrow?" asked Joyce.

"I have a funeral at Mortonhall Crematorium in the afternoon," replied Luke.

"You remember the man in Miller Street who was knocked down by a car a couple of months ago. He died in the Royal Infirmary last week, without ever regaining consciousness. I called round to see his wife the day after it happened. They don't come to church but she seemed to appreciate my visit and asked if I'd go and see her husband in hospital and say a prayer. I've sat with them in the Royal a few times and she'd like me to take the funeral. It'll be a tough one for everyone – he was only in his forties and there are two teenage girls as well. So I'll need to prepare for that in the morning. These are the things that really test people's faith. It's strange, though. At the session meeting Jean Thompson quoted from John chapter 14, where Jesus says that in his Father's house there are many mansions. She asked how that squared with his words, in the same chapter: 'No-one comes to the Father but by me'. She also said that she couldn't believe in a God who loved only the Christians and I suppose that's the breadth the parish minister is trying to represent. My job is to minister to anyone in the parish who wants my services; not just to the paid up members of the congregation."

Sensing a sermon coming on Joyce interjected: "My goodness, look at the time. It's nearly midnight. I'm off to bed. Don't sit up too late."

The funeral was a difficult occasion. Luke hadn't kept a tally of how many he had conducted over thirty years of ministry but each one was unique and he always tried to approach this part of his job in a way that was fresh and not formulaic. As it often fell to him to give the tribute – even though he had never met the deceased – he tried to glean as much detail as he could from the grieving family so he could paint a picture which was both recognisable and affectionate. Humour too had its place, if judged astutely, with a recollection of some particular foible or idiosyncrasy creating smiles and easing tension. Luke had once heard a colleague described as 'not much of a preacher but he does a lovely funeral'. This was an important part of ministry and one to be taken very seriously.

The day following was clear in the diary and, since a divinity student serving a placement was to preach on Sunday, Luke did not have to turn his mind to writing a sermon. Now is my chance, he thought. I'll make a start on reading the *Qur'an*. That will certainly be different.

Luke had already ascertained some basic facts about the *Qur'an*. It was much shorter than the Bible –approximately one-tenth in length, coming in at around 77,000 words compared with the Bible's 775,000. That included the Old Testament with 593,000 and the New Testament at 181,000. So the *Qur'an* is less than half the length of the New Testament. Like the Bible it's divided into chapters, called *suras* meaning literally 'rows'. There are 114 *suras*. Unlike the Bible the *Qur'an* does not comprise a series of books equivalent to *Genesis, Deuteronomy, St Matthew,* etc.

Luke had also learned that the *Qur'an* originated in the seventh century, the tradition being that it had been revealed by God to the Prophet Muhammad through the Angel Gabriel in and around the cities of Mecca and Medina between the years 610 and 632. The word '*Qur'an*' means 'recited' or 'that which is read'. This is why for Muslims the authentic way of engaging with the *Qur'an* is not to read it as one might read the Bible, but to recite it in the original Arabic. For Muslims Arabic is the language of Paradise and all Muslims, whatever their first language, are encouraged to pray, read the *Qur'an* and greet one another in this universal language of Islam. There is particular merit in being able to recite the text from memory. Well, I can't manage that, said Luke to himself. I'll just have to make do with reading an English translation.

But why am I setting myself this task - this challenge even - Luke wondered.

He reminded himself: Jews, Christians and Muslims are referred to as 'people of the book'. That's what the Mufti in Aleppo had said, and all three faiths trace their spiritual origins back to Abraham. I've read the Bible several times, he mused, and that includes the Hebrew Scriptures, which Christians call the Old Testament. I've also studied the specifically Christian writings known as the New Testament.

I suppose that means I've covered two thirds of the book referred to in the phrase, 'people of the book', so now it's time to complete the trilogy.

And over the coming weeks he did just that, finding references to familiar figures from the Bible –Adam and Eve, Noah, Abraham, Joseph, Moses, David and Goliath, Jonah, Jesus and Mary, his mother. One passage, Luke thought, bore a remarkable similarity to St Luke's account of the Annunciation:

> *(And remember) when the angels said: O Mary! Lo! Allah giveth thee glad tidings of a word from him, whose name is the Messiah, Jesus, son of Mary, illustrious in the world and the Hereafter, and one of those brought near (unto Allah). (Q3:45)*

He was struck too by another verse which had Jesus uttering words not unlike those used in the Biblical account of his temptations by the devil:

> *And lo! Allah is my Lord and your Lord. So serve Him. That is the right path. (Q19:36)*

In his reading he even discovered instructions along the lines of nine of the Ten Commandments, the missing one being the command to observe the seventh day as a holy Sabbath.

At the same time Luke noted that, while Jesus was given a respectful place in the *Qur'an*, Christian claims that he was Son of God, along with the notion of a Trinitarian God, were roundly rejected:

> *O People of the Scripture! Do not exaggerate in your religion nor utter aught concerning Allah save the truth. The Messiah, Jesus son of Mary,*

was only a messenger of Allah, and His word
which He conveyed unto Mary, and a spirit from
Him. So believe in Allah and His messengers, and
say not "Three" - Cease! (it is) better for you! -
Allah is only One God. Far is it removed from
His Transcendent Majesty that He should have a
son. His is all that is in the heavens and all that is
in the earth. And Allah is sufficient as Defender.
(Q4:172)

One area about which Luke was curious to learn was *sharia*. The popular perception was that this was a brutal legal system, a hangover from the mediaeval period when thieves had their right hands cut off and women were stoned in the street for adultery. He was interested, therefore, surprised even, to learn that *sharia* is an old Arab word meaning 'pathway to be followed', or 'path to the water hole'. This rather pastoral definition, as Luke found it, reflected the crucial nature of such a path in the desert.

Essentially, Luke learned that *sharia* represented a whole way of life in accordance with the teachings of the *Qur'an* and the accumulated traditions known as the *Sunna or Hadith*. He found particularly helpful something he read which likened *sharia* to the Jewish *Halakhah* code and the Christian concept of *the strait and narrow*. In other words *sharia* was to be seen more as a set of principles for right living than a clearly codified list of rules. However, this meant that, alongside *sharia*, there was a need for a process of interpretation to determine whether particular conduct conformed to *sharia*. This process was known as *fiqh*, a system of jurisprudence seeking to understand and apply the divine will in practical day to day affairs.

Luke also noted that the application of *sharia* varied from country to country, for example, with regard to women covering their heads. At the same time, it was this freedom to vary which allowed for the more notorious examples of *sharia,* such as public stoning and cutting off of hands. Inevitably, such extreme examples found their way into news headlines, around the world and brought into disrepute a system intended to regulate behaviour and relationships within Islamic societies.

Luke was also interested to discover more about the Islamic concept of *jihad,* often translated as 'holy war' and used as a justification for atrocities such as the 9/11 attacks. In the *Qur'an* he read:

> *Sanction is given unto those who fight because they have been wronged; and Allah is indeed able to give them victory;*
>
> *Those who have been driven from their homes unjustly only because they said: Our Lord is Allah - For had it not been for Allah's repelling some men by means of others, cloisters and churches and oratories and mosques, wherein the name of Allah is oft mentioned, would assuredly have been pulled down. Verily Allah helpeth one who helpeth Him. Lo! Allah is Strong, Almighty –*
> *(Q22:39-40)*

Islam grew up in a context of tribal conflict over trade and other issues. Initially Muhammad refused requests by his followers to fight. A story tells of an old woman daily throwing rotting garbage at the Prophet and cursing him. His companions wanted him to take action against her but he would not. One day the woman did not appear and, on learning that she had taken ill, Muhammad went to see her and offered comfort and prayer. However eventually, in face of aggressive rejection and continuing persecution by the people of Mecca, and the threatening of the new Muslim state based in Medina, Muslim tradition records that the above revelation was revealed. Various skirmishes with the Meccans ensued, culminating in the Battle of al-Badr where the Muslims secured a significant victory. This was in the year 624 and is generally reckoned to have been a turning point in the expansion of Islam. Over the next hundred years the new faith would reach Spain in the west and the borders of China and India in the east.

Jesus grew up in a different context but, even so, the Gospel narratives give mixed messages. He rebuked Peter for his violence towards the High Priest's servant in the Garden of Gethsemane. He instructed his followers to turn the other cheek and to love their enemies. Yet he is also recorded as saying he had come to bring fire to the earth and to set father against son, mother against daughter. And his anger at the exploitative traders in the temple turned physical when he overthrew the tables of the money changers. For both faiths, it occurred to Luke, there were challenges in interpreting ancient and sacred texts in their context. What was not in dispute, though, he realised, was the use of military imagery in the New Testament which subsequently found its way into Christian hymnody. For example, the epistle to Ephesians has a famous passage about putting on the whole armour of God, the better to challenge evil and St Paul refers more than once to early church leaders as 'fellow soldiers'. Such language had given rise to popular hymns such as *Onward Christian Soldiers, Stand up Stand up for Jesus* and *Fight the*

Good Fight. Perhaps, Luke mused, there is no more practical illustration of the military analogy than the Salvation Army. Nobody thinks of it as a real army fighting military battles, but in its work of addressing a variety of social evils, and giving practical help to the victims of such evils, it certainly has a fight on its hands.

But for people of faith there is also the inner, personal struggle with the demons of temptation to stray from the *strait and narrow* and, on further study, Luke learned that the Islamic concept of *jihad* could also be understood in this sense of spiritual discipline. Indeed, for Muslims this is seen as the greater *jihad.* Once again he saw connections and parallels with Christian practices down the centuries such as prayer, fasting and self-denial. Did not both Lent and Ramadan, he reflected, call for similar disciplines in pursuit of a holy life, with God rather than self at the centre?

And yet the more literal interpretation of fighting the good fight could not be written out of the story. Luke remembered from his Church history how a turning point came when the Emperor Constantine, believing that the sign of the cross in the sky had gained him victory in battle, immediately became a Christian. From that point onwards the Church became aligned with secular powers and the line from another hymn 'Take up thy Cross, take up thy sword and fight the battles of the Lord', represented a military reality, not just a forceful metaphor. Undeniably the history of the Church contained many incidents where Christians had taken up the sword - the Crusades, the Inquisition, the Reformation period, Scotland's covenanting wars and today's continuing scourge of sectarianism. Equally, the acting out of *jihad* as holy war was all too evident in such events as the 9/11 attacks on the

United States. How then are the 'people of the book' to relate to one another today? Can they co-operate in the cause of peace or must their divisions and disagreement continue to multiply the world's woes?

These were the questions which Luke's reading led him to ponder. He reflected how while the term 'Islam' literally means 'submission' or 'surrender' (to God) it also has the same root as the Arabic word meaning 'peace' - *Salaam*. This gives rise to the common Muslim greeting, *Salaam Alaikum*, meaning 'peace be with you'. In turn *Salaam* is very similar to the Hebrew word *Shalom*, which also means 'peace' and is a common Jewish greeting. And, when Christians gather to share in their central act of worship, the Eucharist, the liturgy traditionally includes an opportunity for people to look their neighbours in the eye, shake hands and exchange the words, 'Peace be with you'.

What happened to all this peace, Luke wondered, and how can we truly live it out together?

6

Over the coming weeks and months Luke continued on his project of reading the *Qur'an* as time and parish duties allowed. He also read more generally on the subject of Islam. For example, he was interested to understand the distinction between *Sunni* and *Shia* and to what extent there might be some equivalence to Christian differences such as Catholic, Orthodox and Protestant.

In church history classes at college he had learned of the great split in 1054 when the Christian Church had divided on East/West, Orthodox/Catholic lines, the two halves centred respectively on Constantinople and Rome. Then five hundred years later a further schism occurred within the western Church, as some embraced the Reformation movement led by people like Martin Luther, while others maintained allegiance to the Pope. These were the broad fault lines but, within these were further differences of theology and practice. Scotland was a particularly good example. Under the leadership of men such as John Knox the Scots embraced the Reformation in 1560. However, the ensuing century saw a Church, not only reformed, but divided between presbyterian and episcopalian sympathisers. When, around the turn of the seventeenth and eighteenth centuries, separate presbyterian and episcopal denominations eventually emerged, it was not long before further splits arose, particularly within the presbyterian tradition. Even at the beginning of the twenty-first century, Luke estimated, there were around half a dozen presbyterian denominations in Scotland. He recalled an old joke about a Scottish presbyterian who was rescued after being stranded for many years on a desert island. His rescuers observed that he had passed the time by building not just one but two churches on the island. "Why two?" they asked. Pointing to each in turn the man replied: "That's the one I go to and that's the one I don't go to on principle."

Luke was interested therefore to learn the *Sunni/Shia* distinction went right back to the earliest days of Islam and arose from a disagreement as to who should succeed to the leadership following Muhammad's death. At the time of that occurrence there was already a community of some 100,000 Muslims on the Arabian Peninsula. During the Prophet's final illness the honour of leading the prayers had been given to his close companion, Abu Bakr. From this the great majority accepted him as the chosen leader. However, a smaller group believed that the Prophet had appointed his son-in-law and cousin, Ali, as successor and sole interpreter of his legacy. The supporters of Abu Bakr's succession prevailed and they became known as the *Sunnis* since they were seen as following the '*Sunna*', which means the word of the Prophet. The supporters of Ali lost out and were known as *Shia*, a contraction of the phrase *Shiat Ali* meaning 'supporter of Ali'. To this day one of the key differences between *Sunni* and *Shia* is that, for the former, authority is vested in the *Qur'an* and the handed down commentary and tradition known as the *Sunna* or *Hadith*. Meantime, for *Shia* authority is focussed on the Prophet and his descendants, human beings especially chosen by God to represent him on earth. At the present time 85% of the world's Muslims are *Sunni*. The main *Shii* populations are found in Iran and Iraq, with significant minority *Shii* communities in Yemen, Bahrain, Syria and Lebanon. Around 96% of British Muslims are *Sunni* with just 2% *Shia*.

In his reading Luke also discovered a number of facts of which he had not previously been aware:

- More than twice as many Muslims speak Indonesian, Bengali or Urdu as speak Arabic.
- There are significant Muslim populations in religiously plural societies, for example, India, China, Nigeria, Sudan, Lebanon, the Balkans and Malaysia. This means that many Muslims do not live in Muslim majority countries.
- Non-Arab Muslims vastly out number Arab Muslims.
- At the present time 33% of the world population is Christian, with 22% Muslim. By the end of the 21st century, on present trends, it is estimated that together Christians and Muslim will represent 66% of world population – a good reason for seeking out ways of co-operation and paths of peace, Luke reckoned.

As amongst Christian denominations there is a shared recognition of the Bible as a central and sacred text, so all Muslims honour and respect the *Qur'an*. However, as with the churches, it is in matters of interpretation and application that differences arise. For example, just as Christian theology envisages a second coming of Christ so Muslims anticipate the end of time being ushered in by the appearance of the *Mahdi*. Indeed a verse in the *Qur'an* links the two when it talks of *Isa* (Jesus) being a sign for the coming of the hour of judgement (Q43:63). This thought is further developed in a *Sunni hadith* which envisages *Isa* (Jesus) descending at the point of a white arcade east of Damascus and joining with the *Mahdi* to unite humanity. In *Shii* tradition the *Mahdi* will be a reincarnation of the ninth century twelfth imam (after Muhammad), Muhammad al-Mahdi, who, according to tradition, did not die but was taken into concealment by God. Not all *Sunnis* accept the *Mahdi* doctrine, but for those who do the *Mahdi* is yet to be born. Reading about these differing beliefs Luke found himself making comparisons with Christian teaching on the ascension of Christ and his rule at God's right hand, until he comes again to judge the living and the dead. He also reflected on connections with Christ's teaching on the Kingdom of God and the phrase from the Lord's Prayer – *thy Kingdom come, thy will be done in earth as it is in heaven.* He also remembered the expectation of a Messiah, which was such a prominent theme in the Hebrew Scriptures and how, for Christians, Jesus was this predicted Messiah. This then led him to reflect on how Muslims had their holy book, the *Qur'an* and, alongside it, other sacred texts known as the *Sunna* or *Hadith.* Was there an equivalence here to Christians acknowledging authority in Creeds, Confessions, doctrinal statements, decisions of Church Councils and Assemblies over the centuries of Christian history, as well as in the Bible? In Luke's own church, the Church of Scotland, the Bible is recognised as 'supreme rule of faith and life', while a seventeenth document, known as the Westminster Confession of Faith, has the status of 'subordinate standard.' Luke had often wondered whether the twenty-first century church was well served by such interpretations of Scripture from another age. He was interested therefore to discover that within Islam a similar debate was taking place over how to be faithful to ancient traditions without becoming trapped in the past, still less trying to recreate the past.

There were also practical level differences between *Shia* and *Sunni*, Luke noted. For example the *Sunni* pattern is to pray five times a day while *Shia* may combine certain prayers enabling them to pray just three times each day. In *Sunni* Islam the imam's role is simply to lead the prayers; for *Shia* the imam has authority to instruct in the faith. *Shii* practice thus allows for a degree of hierarchy in its leadership which is not the way with *Sunnis*. That's definitely something I can identify with as a presbyterian, smiled Luke. Indeed, it's probably the most obvious outward difference between catholic and episcopal organisation on the one hand, and presbyterian and congregationalist structures on the other. He recalled how one of his professors at college would stress the importance for the Kirk of the principle of parity of ministers – adding with a twinkle in his eye: "always remembering, of course, that some are more equal than others!"

It was as he was immersed in reading about such matters that his studies were interrupted by the ringing of the telephone. He and Joyce had recently bought new telephone handsets which let you see the number of the incoming call. It was a number which Luke immediately recognised – Head Office - though, given the flat structure of the Church of Scotland, such hierarchical language was frowned upon. The call was indeed from the central offices of the Church in Edinburgh and the caller was the Rev Sandra Kilgour who headed up the Kirk's ecumenical and interfaith work. It was she who had approached Luke the previous year following his article in *Ministers' Forum* and sounded him out about accompanying the Moderator to Syria and Lebanon.

"Good morning, Luke," she began briskly. "Thanks, again for being a member of the Middle East delegation. It all seemed to go well and we've had good feedback from the Moderator and also from the church people there. Of course things are pretty tense now that the bombing of Iraq has begun, but all the more important that we should keep the communications channels open."

"I quite agree," responded Luke. "It was a privilege to be part of the group and thank you again for asking me. I wouldn't have missed it for anything. A couple of weeks ago I gave a fairly full account of the visit to my kirk session and it prompted a good discussion. Inevitably I suppose, there was some negative comment about whether this was the best use of the Moderator's time. At the same time, though, there were strong voices saying that we need to work harder on establishing good interfaith relations right here in Scotland."

"Music to my ears," said Sandra, "and that's really what I'm phoning about. Have you heard of the Scottish Interfaith Council?"

"Well I've heard of it, but that's about all I can say," answered Luke.

"It's quite a new body, set up just three years ago in 2000 as a means of encouraging dialogue between Scotland's various religious communities. The Church of Scotland has signed up to it and we're looking for someone to represent us over the next four years. Your name came up and I'm phoning to ask if you would think about it."

Well, to cut to the chase, Luke did think about it – quite a bit. He discussed it with Joyce and with Brian, his session clerk, in effect, the leading member of the congregation. Wise ministers don't spring surprises on their session clerks. Brian, worrying about how much of Luke's time might be required and consequent implications for his time in the parish, asked what the duties were. Joyce, knowing that her husband sometimes felt rather hemmed in by parochial demands (in both senses of the word), thought it was a great opportunity for him to 'swim in a bigger sea' as she put it; though she warned that it might bring its own frustrations.

"Well, at least fresh frustrations are a change from familiar ones," Luke observed, giving expression to his cynical side; though if Joyce had used the word he would have claimed he was simply being realistic.

In the end he decided to accept and try to play his part in fostering friendship amongst the members of Scotland's diverse cultural and religious communities. Clearly all this reading up on Islam had been for a purpose, and it was certainly to come in very useful over the next few years. During that time Luke attended regular and routine meetings of the Interfaith Council and, in this regard, Joyce had been spot on. For every agenda with opportunities for discussing matters of belief and spirituality there was an agenda dealing with budgetary and staffing issues, risk assessments, health and safety regulations and all the usual bread and butter matters with which organisations have to deal. At least it's novel, decided Luke, to be working on budget priorities with Hindus, Jews, Muslims, Buddhists, Baha'is and Sikhs. That's certainly different from Capelaw kirk session or meetings of the local presbytery.

But there was high level stuff too. The Council serviced the regular meetings of faith leaders and Luke attended some of these. He recalled one amusing moment on his way to such a meeting at Glasgow's Central Mosque. For ease of identity he had decided to go formally attired wearing a clerical collar. He hailed a cab at Glasgow's Queen Street station and, in response to the cabbie's "Where to?", replied "The Central Mosque, please." The driver, who had by this point engaged gear returned the gear stick to neutral, paused, turned round and commented: "That's not what I was expecting you to say, Sir".

Luke smiled, observed that times were changing and then briefly outlined the work of the Council.

"Good on you," said the cabbie. "There's far too much fighting and killing going on. Just because someone's a different religion doesn't mean they're an enemy".

"How about you come to the meeting with me?" smiled Luke.

"I don't think so," replied the cabbie. "I'm not a great one for meetings and I've got a living to make."

"Fair enough," said Luke, "each to their own, but I'll certainly pass on your comments."

Another meeting was held on Holy Island, a Buddhist retreat centre off the larger island of Arran in the Firth of Clyde. This was hosted by the genial and irrepressible Lama Yeshe Losal, the Abbot of the Samye Ling Centre at Eskdalemuir who as a young man had walked across the Himalayas to escape persecution in Tibet. The meeting was residential, with ample time for quiet and meditation. Indeed, after 8 p.m. the only options were a walk round the island or retiring for the night – no question of a convivial drink in the bar, as was usually the form at ecumenical conferences. The next morning's meditation was also a challenge. Luke was in awe of the way the Buddhists could sit on the floor for an hour without even twitching. He, meanwhile, hadn't realised how many bits of his body could simultaneously develop infuriating itches in such a short time. But conversations were good. He met a Buddhist nun whose mother was a Church of Scotland elder.

"What made you become a Buddhist?" Luke had asked.

Her answer contained a negative and a positive: a growing dissatisfaction with the wordiness of traditional church worship and an exposure to meditation while at university. She remained on good terms with her family and, it emerged, both she and Luke shared a favourite hymn: *Immortal, Invisible, God only wise*, with its celebration of a God who lives in all things.

Other meetings, too, had lodged in Luke's memory, and not always for religious reasons. One of the best curries he had ever tasted was served up when the faith leaders met at the Hindu Mandir in Glasgow; though he was sure the discussion had also been excellent. More poignantly he remembered a meeting at the Baha'i Centre in Edinburgh where, in a time of quietness, members of the group had prayed, each in his or her own way, for Baha'i victims of brutal oppression and persecution in Iran. He often thought of this when people expressed concern about 'interfaith worship.' They would say things like: "I'm open to interfaith dialogue but I have a real problem with interfaith worship – that's a compromise too far."

Luke recognised that interfaith worship certainly posed challenges. Christian hymns could present a problem for people of other faiths; equally to censor such hymns would offend Christian sensitivities, suggesting they were ashamed or embarrassed by affirmations of God's saving grace in Christ. There was no easy answer to this but what was certainly possible, in Luke's view, was for people from different religions to gather together in one place and offer up prayer in their own ways. This is what Luke had done when he attended the Abu Nour Mosque in Damascus with the Moderator and his party. He had reasoned: If God can hear my prayers in Capelaw Parish Church and in the quietness of my study he can surely hear them in a Syrian mosque. How, he had wondered, can showing respect to a Muslim community undermine the legitimacy of my own beliefs or devalue what God has done in Jesus Christ? And as he continued to think about this he remembered a hymn they often sang at Capelaw, *There's a wideness in God's mercy.* This had been a favourite of his old 'bishop', the *Qur'an* reading Edward Bryan and Luke remembered every time they sang it Edward grumbled that the hymn book version omitted what he thought was the most important verse:

> *But we make his love too narrow*
> *By false limits of our own;*
> *And we magnify his strictness*
> *With a zeal he will not own.*

Luke duly served out his four year term on the Interfaith Council and on one occasion was a member of a delegation which met Scotland's First Minister to discuss issues of concern to all faith groups. What he observed was that, while different bodies had different agendas, there was always an underlying commonality, just through being people of faith. Sometimes this showed itself in unexpected ways. For example it happened more than once when Christianity appeared to be under attack. One incident concerned the defacing of old Bibles in an exhibition, another when a worker was ordered not to wear a cross-shaped necklace to work. After such stories appeared in the newspapers Luke would invariably receive a phone call or e-mail, perhaps from a Sikh or Jewish member of the Council, to express sympathy and solidarity. It was as though an attack on one religious tradition was an attack on all.

Towards the end of Luke's term he was particularly pleased when an invitation came to the Convener of the Council to address the General Assembly. An Orthodox Jew, Diana Wolfson was only the second person from another religion to address the Assembly, the first being another Jew, Dr Henry Tankel, back in 1984. Mrs Wolfson made clear she was speaking on this occasion on behalf of the Interfaith Council. This was in 2007 and her core message was that, while different religions had varying beliefs and rituals they shared common values such as charity, loving kindness, peace and caring for the weak and the vulnerable. Her words were well received, as was her personal story of growing up as a member of the only Jewish family in a West Lothian village. There her father had been the doctor and a close friend of both the parish minister and the Roman Catholic priest. Accompanying Mrs Wolfson was a colourful delegation drawn from Scotland's diverse faith communities. When asked by the Moderator to stand and be recognised they were greeted with generous applause.

Another development which delighted Luke was the decision by the Church of Scotland to appoint a part time Interfaith Officer. This struck him as an imaginative step, though he had feared that financial pressures might have forced it down the priority ranking. His pleasure was increased when, in the report explaining the desirability of the post, he spied a reference to the World Council of Church's San Antonio Declaration. He recalled quoting that to the kirk session on his return from Syria: *We cannot point to any other way of salvation than Jesus Christ; at the same time we cannot set limits to the saving power of God.*

Not only was Luke pleased to see this. He was even more delighted to see that the authors of the report had included a fuller extract from the Declaration:

Our ministry of witness among people of other faiths presupposes our presence with them, sensitivity to their deepest faith commitments and experiences, willingness to be their servants for Christ's sake, affirmation of what God has done and is doing among them, and love for them. Since God's mystery in Christ surpasses our understanding and since our knowledge of God's saving power is imperfect, we Christians are called to be witnesses to others, not judges of them. We also affirm that it is possible to be non-aggressive and missionary at the same time – that is, in fact, the only way of being truly missionary.

Looking back over his four year term on the Scottish Interfaith Council Luke recognised that it had been an enriching and mind broadening experience. He was genuinely sorry when the time came for him to be replaced, but his sorrow was eased by the realisation that what had begun as contacts with followers of other religions had developed into friendships and that these would endure. The blow was further softened by an agenda item at his final meeting of the Council which was to prove the truth of the saying that when one door closes another opens. The agenda item was 'Proposed Scottish Interfaith Pilgrimage'.

It emerged that a small group of individuals, drawn from the Christian, Jewish and Muslim faiths, had got together and were organising an interfaith visit to Israel and Palestine. Their thinking was that Jerusalem was holy and a place of pilgrimage for all three religions. The Western Wall of Solomon's temple, also known as the 'Wailing Wall' was where Jews gathered for prayer, the crevices in the ancient stonework often stuffed with pieces of paper with supplications written on them.

Luke recalled the Christian pilgrimage in which he had taken part some years previously. At the time a young Israeli soldier had been kidnapped by a Palestinian group which was threatening to kill him unless ransom demands were met. Luke and some of his party had decided to take an evening walk through the old city from their hotel by the Damascus Gate and soon found themselves in the great square by the Western Wall. There an agitated crowd had gathered, bobbing up and down in furious prayer.

"What's going on?" Luke asked a bystander who was obviously a tourist.

"The deadline for executing that soldier is approaching and people are getting restless. We're just heading back to our hotel and you might want to think about doing the same."

And they did. On arrival back at the hotel Luke found a message to say his wife had phoned. Mobile phones weren't so widely used then and certainly not overseas.

"Where have you been?" Joyce enquired when Luke returned the call.

"Oh, some of us took a walk down to the Western Wall," he replied.

"You what!" exclaimed Joyce. "I've just been watching the scene on the BBC News. It looks really ugly."

"Yes it was threatening to get a bit lively," replied Luke, "but don't worry, we're back in the hotel now."

"Well, just be careful. You know I was quite anxious about you going to Israel, what with suicide bombers and angry protests."

"I know," said Luke, "but it's been tense here for three thousand years and I think it's important for ministers to see the places they speak about in sermons every Sunday."

"I know, I know," said Joyce, resignedly and so the conversation turned to family matters.

As well as the Western Wall Jerusalem contains the Temple Mount with the striking golden Dome of the Rock. Alongside sits the silver topped *Al Aqsa* Mosque, the whole complex constituting *al-Haram ash-Sharif* (The Noble Sanctuary), whither the Prophet made his famous night journey and whence he ascended into heaven. Here is Islam's third holiest site after the *Kabah* at Mecca and the Prophet's Mosque at Medina. There were also many places of Christian pilgrimage in the city – the Mount of Olives with the Garden of Gethsemane at its foot, the *Via Dolorosa* (the Way of the Cross) and the Church of the Holy Sepulchre, traditional site of the crucifixion. All these were places of pilgrimage for followers of the three faiths, but what was now being proposed was a shared pilgrimage. Christians, Muslims and Jews could act as guides one to another in an exploration of their holy places. This way differences could be explored within a context of shared enterprise and friendship.

So, at Luke's last meeting as a member of the Scottish Interfaith Council this idea was tabled for discussion and with an invitation to members of the Council to take part. There was a general welcome for the proposal, though the treasurer, as treasurers do, cautioned that the Council itself could not contribute much in the way of funding assistance. That would need to come from the participating faith bodies. A Baha'i member pointed out that their principal shrine was in Haifa and she would be very keen to participate in the pilgrimage.

She would also be happy to arrange a visit to the shrine of the Bab and the lovely gardens in which it was situated. Luke also expressed support in principle and wondered whether the Church of Scotland guesthouse in Jerusalem and the Scots Hotel in Tiberias might accommodate the pilgrims during their stay. And so it was left to the officials of the Council to talk further with the organisers and for individuals to consider their own possible participation. The proposed dates were more than a year away so there was plenty of time.

7

Luke had gone home from that Interfaith Council meeting quite full of the idea but, recalling Joyce's anxiety about his last visit to one of the world's main hotspots, he had been apprehensive about mentioning it. He need not have worried. Not only did Joyce think it was a great idea she wondered whether they might both take part.

"I've never been to the Holy Land," she observed, "and this sounds like a particularly interesting way to do it. It'll probably be no holiday but, if there's space, let's do it instead of a summer holiday next year. And, when all's said and done, I'd rather be with you there than worrying at home."

So over the ensuing months arrangements were made by the organisers. Luke enquired about church accommodation and this was offered at a favourable rate. Passport details of all those taking part were sent to the Israeli Embassy in London with a view to facilitating visas for those who might need them. Funding was secured from charitable bodies and the Scottish Government and this enabled subsidised places to be offered, particularly to younger people. The First Minister even wrote a letter encouraging and commending the project. A guide was secured, an Israeli deeply committed to the peace process who was well regarded on both sides of the political and religious divide and who had all the right contacts to open the doors through which the pilgrims wished to pass.

So eventually, on a bright July afternoon in the summer of 2008 a motley and colourful group gathered at Edinburgh Airport for the short flight to Amsterdam, then onwards to Tel-Aviv. In total the party numbered thirty, drawn from seven faith communities – Baha'i, Buddhist, Christian, Hindu, Jewish, Muslim and Sikh. As hoped the group included a good number of under-30s from across the religious spectrum. Spirits were high and the Schiphol layover was further enlivened by large screen broadcasts of the Wimbledon Federer-Nadal final. Tantalisingly the match was tied at two sets each when it was time to board. (Nadal won the fifth and so the championship.) However, the mood slumped shortly after arrival into Tel-Aviv's Ben Gurion Airport in the small hours of the morning. There the pilgrims had their first encounter with the realities of what they were getting into. Despite having an official letter from the Israeli Embassy in London confirming everyone's passport details five members of the group - all Muslims - were taken aside for questioning. This delayed things for less than an hour but it was an unsettling start. However, once the group was reunited on the waiting coach and began to process the experience, positive aspects were acknowledged: for example the concern felt by those waved through for those who had been treated differently, and the sporting recognition by those questioned that the security people had an important job to do in keeping everyone safe. The effect of such mutual sympathy served only to strengthen and unify the group. There were also wry smiles when Luke told how he had sought to explain the pilgrimage's aim of bringing people from different faiths and cultures together. The security official's response had been a puzzled look accompanied by the single word, "Why?"

"Clearly she thinks we're crazy," Luke remarked. "Perhaps we are," a voice from the back of the bus added.

For Luke there was another positive aspect to the delay. It meant that they approached Jerusalem - most for the first time - as the sun was rising, its radiance reflected magnificently from the golden Dome of the Rock, just across the Kedron Valley from the Mount of Olives. He remarked to Joyce (she had indeed come along) that on the same journey in his previous visit, at the same time of day, the coach driver had stopped in a layby which afforded magnificent views of the city. There the leader of the group had read the pilgrim Psalm 122: "I was glad when they said unto me, let us go up to the house of the Lord . . . Pray for the peace of Jerusalem."

And so they arrived at the guesthouse. The sun was by then well up but a few short hours of sleep were called for. From their room Luke and Joyce could look across to the Jaffa Gate of the old city and as they did so Luke reflected on what an ideal location this was – close to the green line which separated Jewish west Jerusalem from Arab east Jerusalem. The guest house was attached to St Andrew's Scots Memorial Church, which had been built on this site in the years after the First World War. Paid for by public subscription it was dedicated as a Memorial to Scots who had fought and died in Palestine. Under a succession of ministries the church had maintained a Christian witness on what had become a political and religious fault-line, and sought to play its part in not only praying but working for the peace of Jerusalem.

After a couple of hours of fitful sleep it was time for the group to reassemble for a first meal together – a late breakfast/ early lunch. It sounded so simple and straightforward, but it soon emerged that this was not the case. The group's requirements called for kosher, halal and vegetarian and the guesthouse had considerable experience of meeting such expectations. However, it was also necessary for the Jews to have their own crockery and cutlery and the simplest way to manage this was to seat the Jews together at their own table. This was not an auspicious start, for it seemed to cut right across the whole purpose of the group, at the same time highlighting at the most basic level the challenges of cross-cultural community living. It was therefore further evidence of the good will already engendered that a solution was soon found. Future meals would be self-serve buffet style with disposable plates and cutlery laid out. People could then choose appropriately from the dishes on offer and sit at any table alongside any member of the party.

At one level this might seem trivial and annoying but, again, it underlined the challenge which lay at the heart of the whole project, namely, how to live with and respect difference. At the end of the day, Luke pondered, the aim of interfaith dialogue is to learn about the beliefs and customs of others and recognise that, even if you think these are silly or just plain wrong, they are as important to the other person as your faith and practice is to you. It also underscored the point that the main outcomes of the pilgrimage would be its effect on the pilgrims in terms of mutual understanding and acceptance. Nobody had any illusions that a possible outcome might be a sudden and dramatic emergence of peace in the Middle East! At best the example of such diverse individuals enjoying one another's company might give a message to some with whom the group met. There was also the prospect of a 'trickle down' effect back in Scotland as the participants shared their experience and new cross-cultural friendships were maintained. So a resolution to the food question which respected what lay behind it was an important first step, as it was it was to prove again later in the week when provision had to be made for non-meat eaters sharing a Shabbat meal following Friday evening prayers at Jerusalem's Great Synagogue.

In planning the visit the organisers had been clear from the start that the focus should be on faith, not politics, while recognising that disentangling the two was never going to be easy. A good example of the difficulty was a visit to the tomb of the Patriarchs in Hebron. Given Abraham's importance for Jews and Muslims this is a sacred place for both faiths and the tomb itself lies at the heart of a complex which has a synagogue at one side and a mosque at the other. Hebron itself, situated in the West Bank, is home to 250,000 Palestinians and around 1,000 Jewish settlers. Memories of a 1929 massacre of Jews and a 1994 massacre of Palestinians live on, making the city a tense place. On the day of the visit those who were neither Jew nor Muslim divided themselves, with half accompanying the Jews and the other half accompanying the Muslims. Once inside it was possible to look from the mosque into the synagogue and vice versa through a bullet proof glass screen. This sense of separation and alienation was reinforced in a meeting with an armed settler leader whose vision of a two state solution was for Israel to take possession of the whole land and for the Palestinians to find a new homeland somewhere else – anywhere else. Needless to say a rather different perspective was offered when the group visited a Palestinian family living in the shadow of a Jewish settlement.

Luke realised that this divergence of opinion was of a rather different order from the issue over food, utensils and sharing tables at that first meal together in Jerusalem. He had reasoned there that the trick was to respect those who attached great religious significance to customs and beliefs you might struggle with but, now he thought, perhaps that can only go so far. For example, was it reasonable that people be asked to respect those who, if allowed to act on their beliefs, would cause great damage and distress to other human beings? And it wasn't simply a matter of separating out the religion from the politics. The settler perspective offered to the group certainly argued for a political way forward, but the politics was based on a firm religious belief that God had given all the land which comprises modern Israel and Palestine to the Jews 3,000 years ago.

From his Old Testament theology Luke had learned the importance of the Promised Land to the Jewish people, in history and in the present day. From his experience of interfaith dialogue he had learned to respect the right of faith communities to interpret their own sacred texts for themselves. And now, brought face to face with the tensions of the modern West Bank, he was not alone amongst the pilgrim group in being troubled by the depth of the crisis and the scale of the task facing those charged with taking forward a genuine peace process.

The drive back to Jerusalem was, therefore, a sombre affair as people tried to process what they had seen and heard during the course of a long, hot day. A rabbi in the group spoke of the last time he had visited Hebron, thirty-three years previously as a boy of seven. He remembered visiting the holy sites without any fear. He recalled strolling through the Arab *souk*, and buying and haggling with the sellers, all with a smile and banter. Then something happened to both societies, leaving issues so complex and so painful that sometimes reconciliation seemed well-nigh impossible. This struck a chord with everyone. They knew that they were coming to a place of divisions; now they had seen these divisions close-up and it was deeply depressing.

But their guide had a plan and that was to begin with despair and move on to signs of hope. A visit to the Holy Land Trust in Bethlehem set a different tone. Its Palestinian founder had grown up amidst the violence of the occupied territories, but was deeply committed to promoting non-violence both as a principle and a practical strategy. He had even visited Auschwitz and Birkenau concentration camps to see for himself and better appreciate the horrors which the Jewish people had suffered prior to the creation of the State of Israel. As a Palestinian he had felt that was an important step to take since a common Palestinian response to the Holocaust was that, while not responsible for it, they, amongst the peoples of the word, were particularly affected by its legacy. The group heard, for example, that Israeli children can come away from a visit to the Nazi death camps with the impression that this is how the Palestinians would like to treat them.

On the evening of that visit, back in the Church of Scotland guesthouse, the group learned something altogether more hopeful. Their guide had arranged for a prominent group of religious leaders - Christian, Jewish and Muslim – to meet the Scottish interfaith group. What was particularly noteworthy was that this was the first time these individuals had shared a platform. All spoke of their commitment to reconciliation and referred to a meeting soon to be held with Israeli and Palestinian education ministers, with the aim of removing negative stereotyping from school text books. A Muslim Mufti shared a moving personal story. He recalled growing up in Jerusalem pre-1948 when Jews, Christians and Muslims could live and move about freely. At the time, due to circumstances which had arisen, his grandmother had breast-fed a Jewish neighbour's baby. After the formation of the State of Israel the Mufti's uncle had gone abroad to study, but when he tried to return he was denied entry unless he could demonstrate that his family had done some good for the Jewish people. He told the story of his grandmother wet-nursing the Jewish baby, which was authenticated, and was allowed to return.

In the course of the pilgrimage members of the group were to hear other stories of cross cultural friendship and cooperation. One of the most moving of these involved an Israeli father and mother (not husband and wife) both of whom had children who were victims of suicide bombings. One had been killed; the other had been horribly injured but had recovered, thanks to the skill and care of a Palestinian surgeon. When he heard this Luke remembered an incident from some years back when a Jewish student from Glasgow had been killed in a Jerusalem suicide bombing. His grief-stricken parents had not hesitated when the question arose of a sick Palestinian youth receiving a life-saving organ transplant.

The sense of community grew stronger as the group visited historical sites and living communities in Jerusalem and Galilee, in Ramallah, Bethlehem and Haifa. In the last mentioned they moved beyond the predominant Christian/Jewish/Muslim religions to the spiritual home of the Baha'i faith, the beautiful shrine of the Bab, set amidst lush gardens cascading down to the Mediterranean Sea. As a gesture of welcome all members of the group were permitted to enter the shrine, something normally permitted only to Baha'is.

While, as originally conceived, the focus was primarily on religious difference and dialogue time was still taken to engage in a very limited way with the politics. So meetings were also held at the Knesset in Jerusalem and the home of the Palestine authority in Ramallah. Inevitably it was not easy for the Jews and the Muslims to listen to narratives contrary to their own understandings and sympathies. And on one occasion the whole group was challenged when an influential Palestinian academic opined that interfaith dialogue was 'elitist, eclectic and sporadic' and did little to make any practical difference to the lives of those caught up in sectarian conflict. Indeed, this had been a criticism from the outset, to be faced again in post-pilgrimage media interviews which suggested the enterprise was nothing more than a fancy holiday. Christians and Muslims in the group also had to deal with criticism from pro-Palestinian groups in Scotland that the whole thing was just an Israeli inspired PR stunt. In response they pointed out that, were that the case, it certainly didn't work since all members seemed to find things to criticise and commend on both sides of that sad divide.

Someone observed that the group's aims were laudable but muddled. Certainly as Luke thought about it afterwards a great muddle of memories came flooding back – highs and lows, tears and laughter, despair and hope. One particular memory which would long remain was at the lighter end of the spectrum, but also powerfully symbolic. Having arranged the accommodation he felt a degree of responsibility for the group's behaviour. So it was with some anxiety that he realised one night that the distant singing wasn't part of a dream but was coming from downstairs in the Jerusalem guest house. A glance at his watch indicated that it was a little after midnight and, knowing that the interfaith pilgrims were not the only residents, he put on a dressing gown and went to investigate. There, in the lounge, he discovered all the young folk gathered round the piano– Baha'i, Christian, Jewish, Muslim and Sikh – all singing, literally, from the same hymn-sheet. Part of Luke just wanted to join in. But discretion and sensitivity to other guests prevailed: "Great party guys, but it's time for bed."

Another outstanding memory which remained was the final event of the visit. That was attendance by the whole group at the Sunday morning service in St. Andrew's Church, Jerusalem with a representative of each faith making a contribution - a reading, a song, a meditation. All were given a Christian and neighbourly welcome by the minister and regular worshippers, some of whom had journeyed through the nearby security wall for the service. It fell to Luke to preach the sermon, a task which he approached with a sense of its significance but also of challenge.

Here is the text of the sermon Luke preached.

Genesis 25: 19-34; Matthew 13: 1-9, 18-23

It is a great privilege to preach in this beautiful and significant church this morning. I have worshipped here before while on Christian pilgrimage to the Holy Land. This time I am part of a different kind of pilgrimage – what we are calling an interfaith pilgrimage – though I recently found myself having a conversation as to whether 'multi-faith' might be a more appropriate title. My own preference is for 'interfaith' because it suggests more than people from different religions doing the same things at the same time. For me the experience of the past week has been more than that – connections have been made, relationships, indeed friendships have been formed. We have not just been many; we have been together. So I prefer 'inter' to 'multi' to describe what we are about.

In my Christian tradition we have a lectionary with Bible readings set down for each Sunday. This means that the passages we read today will be read in churches all round the world. It also means that the preacher has to cover the Bible over a period of years, not just choose the bits he or she likes. What I do find, though, is that the Bible readings for any given Sunday are usually 'spot-on' and that is certainly the case today.

At the present time the lectionary offers a series of readings from the first book of the Bible, the Book of Genesis. These include stories extending over four generations of the patriarchs, whose tomb at Hebron we visited the other day. This is a good starting point because if we go back to Abraham then immediately we find Jews, Muslims and Christians on common ground. Indeed these three world religions are often referred to as the Abrahamic faiths. I have also learned this week from our Baha'i members that their religion also makes connections with Abraham through Ketura who is mentioned later in the Book of Genesis and who, it is thought, he married after the death of Sarah.

So in churches over these past few weeks worshippers have been hearing again the moving story from earlier in Genesis – the story of the rejection of Hagar and Ishmael following the birth of Isaac to Sarah. The surrogate slave girl and her son are sent away, though not without blessing and promise; and in this ancient story people have seen the beginnings of those two races of Jew and Arab –two faiths Judaism and Islam - both descended from Abraham.

In today's reading we heard of the birth of twin boys to Rebekah, Isaac's wife, the first born called Esau, the second born, Jacob. But again within the story we see family tensions. Esau is favoured by his father; Jacob by his mother. In the traditional way the line of descent and blessing would have come down through the first born. In this case, though, there wasn't much in it as the second twin came out holding on to his brother's heel. Anyway, here the tradition didn't effectively apply as Esau, the first-born twin, sold his birth right to his brother for a bowl of stew. So the Jews trace the line back to Isaac and Abraham through Jacob while Esau is regarded as the forbear of the Edomites.

These ancient stories, set in this part of the world, go back some 3,000 and more years. Yet with the passing generations it seems that the tensions between the original siblings, far from being forgotten become multiplied and magnified into increasing suspicion, mistrust, resentment and outright conflict. For us, who both profess and practice faith, this presents a real challenge as people ask: "Is this really the legacy of faith for our world?"

As I thought about this before coming on the pilgrimage I found myself reflecting on how ironic it is that a land called 'holy', and that is particularly holy to three faiths which amongst them account for more than half of the world's population, should be at the centre of so much conflict. More than that even - how ironic that the interfaith tensions present here are replicated all around the world, as synagogues, mosques, churches are vandalised and individuals find themselves vilified and threatened because of their dress, their culture, their beliefs. Is this really the legacy of faith to our world?

Even more discouraging is the fact that such conflict exists not only between different faiths and cultures; it also exists within them. Back home in Scotland we have a depressing history of sectarian conflict within Christianity. A couple of years ago it was a big news story when the Roman Catholic Cardinal and the Church of Scotland Moderator went together to watch a football match between Rangers and Celtic. Does it not say something about what we have done to religion that that should be such a big deal? And while it is not for me to elaborate, the reality is that similar tensions exist between different factions within other religions.

It is against this background which often associates – sadly all too accurately – religion and conflict that we decided to make our pilgrimage. So we came to Jerusalem, to Israel and Palestine, to visit sites holy to three ancient faiths and to one newer faith, the Baha'i religion with its lovely shrine in Haifa. But our pilgrimage is not just a journey to holy places, still less a journey to the past. It is, rather, a journey of growing awareness, a journey of self-discovery, in the company of people of different faiths. It is a journey of discovering something of the rituals and beliefs of those who do not share our faith, but undeniably share our humanity and embrace values such as charity, loving kindness, peace and care for the weak and vulnerable. The fact that such a diverse group representing seven faith traditions can live peacefully and enjoyably together for a week has to be a tiny glimmer of hope for our divided and violent world.

Just as the Genesis reading seems very apt for today, so does the New Testament passage from St Matthew's Gospel. Jesus often taught lessons by telling stories, referred to as 'parables'. This morning we read one of the most famous, the parable of the sower. The farmer scatters the seed which falls onto different types of soil and ground. The result is that it doesn't all take root and grow. So it was with the teaching of Jesus and still today preachers take comfort from the parable when the response to their sermons is less than universal rapture, or even any discernible difference to the lives of those who hear.

When I read the parable again and thought about our pilgrimage it occurred to me that what we have been trying to do is rather like the sower sowing the seed. Our expectations have, I hope, been realistic. This past week is not going to change the world, but it may change us as individuals just a little bit and that change may have knock-on effects as we tell the story of this past week to our friends and communities back home. Indeed there is a sense in which the work really begins when we return to Scotland tomorrow. I already have invitations to speak and write about this experience and so will others, for this has been an experience to share as we strive towards that vision Jesus often described as the Kingdom of God. Other faiths will have a similar vision, namely a state of affairs where God's will is done on earth, as in heaven, and all God's people come to love their neighbours as themselves. And remember in perhaps the most famous of the parables of Jesus the true neighbour was a Samaritan – a good Samaritan– someone from a different tribe and culture.

Let me just share two delightful moments from this amazing week. Last Tuesday leaders from different faith communities met with us at the guesthouse next door. The evening finished with a rabbi member of our group teaching a song. Across from me stood the Armenian Archbishop and the Depute Mufti of Jerusalem, literally singing from the same song sheet and helping each other follow the English words. The other moment was when a Buddhist monk from our group showed me the postcard he had bought to send to the Church of Scotland congregation which worships along the street from his meditation centre.

There is no doubt that interfaith relations pose challenges to us all. I know that within the churches there are those who are suspicious, fearing that basic beliefs are being compromised by even according respect to other beliefs. In reflecting on that challenge I have found very helpful something which has become known as the San Antonio declaration, taking its name from a World Council of Churches conference held in that Texan city some years ago. The declaration affirms that, while Christians can point to no other salvation than Jesus Christ, at the same time they cannot set limits to the saving power of God. What that suggests to me is that it is when we seek to be most true to our own beliefs that we find the confidence to engage with people of different faiths, treating them with respect and recognising what Britain's Chief Rabbi, Jonathan Sacks, in the title of a recent book calls 'The Dignity of Difference'. In other words: Interfaith is not about creating a wishy-washy, syncretistic mish-mash to which we can all sign up. Rather, it is about affirming our own beliefs, but doing so with grace and love; respecting others and seeing difference, not as threat, but as source of enrichment.

We began some 3,000 years ago with tales of sibling rivalry and family conflict, sadly still realities of today's *world, though now with the capacity to wreak untold destruction on the world itself. How vital it is that we continue to sow the seeds of humanity, hope and peace and affirm our common heritage as children of God.*

8

A couple of weeks after Luke and Joyce arrived back from the interfaith pilgrimage their family gathered at the manse in Capelaw to celebrate Joyce's sixtieth birthday. She had not wanted a fuss and had vetoed a grand party, settling instead for a weekend visit by the immediate family.

Daughter Anne had protested: "But Mum that just gives you extra work, which seems a shame on your birthday."

"Not at all," Joyce had countered. "Your dad's getting quite domesticated in his old age. He is offering to cook something 'not too complicated' on Friday evening; we're all going out for a birthday lunch on Saturday and I'm sure we'll muddle through on Sunday. Your father was going to take Sunday off but, after being away for two Sundays with the Israel/ Palestine visit, he's had second thoughts and feels he should show face at church. Typical!"

And so the weekend was arranged.

By now both Anne and Richard had married – Anne, the previous year, to Archie, a lawyer and would-be Labour Party candidate for the Scottish Parliament. They lived life to the full ('chaotic' was the word Joyce favoured) with Anne's teaching and after-school commitments and Archie's legal work and politics. There was also a lively social life to be fitted in. It was a rare occasion indeed if Joyce or Luke phoned and found one of them at home. How did we manage before answering machines, they often remarked.

By contrast Richard and his wife Alison lived a quieter, home based life in the East Neuk of Fife. They had two children - Katie who was nearly three and baby Marcus. Alison, a pharmacist, was currently on maternity leave. Richard was a chartered accountant based in Dundee. He was also treasurer of the local church where Luke had had the privilege of baptising his grandchildren. There had been some slight tension when Archie gave priority to a political event over Marcus' christening, though Anne had attended, albeit arriving late. Fortunately the custom was for baptisms to take place at the end of the service so she had not missed that.

So on the Friday of the birthday weekend they gathered. Richard had taken a half day so they could take a leisurely drive from Fife, with time to settle the children at Granny and Grandpa's house. This was one of those times when Joyce acknowledged that the large manse in which she and Luke 'rattled around' came into its own. The heating costs might be high, and double glazing would be nice, but at least there was plenty of room for the family. It had been several weeks since she and Luke had seen their grandchildren, so she was not surprised to see how much they had both changed. Katie was quite the little girl now and had acquired a larger vocabulary in the interval. Grandpa's taste for blue cheeses was always something of a joke which explained Katie's opening line:

"Hello Granny, hello Grandpa. Are we having smelly cheese for tea?"

"Don't be cheeky, Katie," chided Alison: "Say hello properly to Granny and Grandpa and give them nice cuddles."

"My goodness, how they have both grown!" exclaimed Joyce.

"Oh yes," replied Alison. "I have to warn you Marcus has just started crawling so beware; and, as you have already seen, Katie isn't shy about coming forward. She's due to start playgroup after the holidays and she's certainly ready for it. So am I! But it's good to see you both safely back from the Middle East. It must have been quite a trip."

"Oh yes, it was," replied Joyce. "We'll fill you in later. Suffice to say it had its ups and downs but neither of us would have missed it for the world."

By the time Anne and Archie arrived from Argyll the children had been fed, bathed and were fast asleep.

"Impeccable timing," observed Richard with a nice mingling of waspish and twinkle.

"Oh, we thought we'd allowed ourselves plenty of time but there was an accident on the M8 which held things up. Anyway, we're here now and it's good to see everyone again," Anne rejoined cheerily. "Don't worry. I'll get up when I hear the children in the morning. Katie will enjoy having breakfast with Auntie Anne!"

"Right, let's get you settled in," said Joyce. It's your usual room – opposite the top of the stairs with the view of the Pentlands. Dad's doing his famous lasagne. Shall we plan to eat in half-an-hour?"

Anticipating the 'famous lasagne' Archie and Anne had thought 'Italian' and brought a couple of bottles of quite decent Chianti.

"Good choice," said Richard. We thought 'Italian' too and brought some tasty Mellis' gorgonzola to follow. Hope it's smelly enough for you dad!"

"Hey, it's <u>my</u> birthday weekend," exclaimed Joyce. Do I not get any treats?"

"Don't worry," said Alison. "We thought of that too and went on-line to order some of your favourite Cocoa Black chocolates from Peebles. So we're all set. Happy Families everyone!"

And it was a happy family dinner to kick off a happy family weekend. It was agreed that Luke had excelled himself with the lasagne. Modestly, he brushed aside the compliments, at the same time explaining that the secret lay in the béchamel sauce. The conversation flowed, as did Archie's and Anne's Chianti, as news was exchanged and plans shared. Alison hoped to get back to work part-time after Marcus's first birthday; Richard was in line for a partnership in his CA practice; Anne was taking on guidance responsibilities at school along with her English classes; Archie was on the short list for a Scottish parliamentary seat. "Not a particularly winnable one," he remarked; "but you have to work your passage. It'll be good experience."

Gradually the conversation turned to Luke and Joyce's recent visit to the Holy Land.

"So how was the trip?" asked Anne.

"Not 'trip' dear, 'pilgrimage – interfaith pilgrimage', if you don't mind," replied Luke, slightly testily.

"Well, all right – pilgrimage," responded Anne. "How was it?"

"It was a very good experience – quite different from my visit to Syria a few years ago. There we were part of friendly meetings between Christians and Muslims. We had some of that this time, but the tensions were more apparent. Perhaps this is understandable, given the continuing failure to achieve a genuine Israeli-Palestinian peace settlement. It was also good to have Mum along to share the experience. That also means we have been able to process it together since we got back."

"Well I think the pilgrimage was a great idea," said Archie.

"There's a significant Muslim population in my prospective constituency and while everyone seems to get along together it's more on a basis of co-existence than integration, or even mutual engagement, of communities. There is still a sense of 'them' and 'us'. I met with a local imam recently and he said that every time there is a Taliban attack on British troops in Afghanistan his people get edgy. He added that his people have no time either for the Taliban, but it's not easy to get that message across to the mass circulation media."

"I see that a bit in school too," said Anne." In fact only a few weeks ago some of our Muslim pupils felt threatened when the older brother of a classmate was killed in Helmand. Mercifully such things are rare but the situation took a bit of managing. That apart, though, I would say that even in the short time I have been teaching things are getting better. Groups of friends include pupils from different ethnic backgrounds and racist incidents are very rare. I feel a bit sorry for the school chaplain, though. Recently he involved some Muslim pupils in reading passages from the *Qur'an* at Assembly and was given a hard time by the Scripture Union members. They thought he was letting the side down. He maintained that the passages which had been read were entirely consistent with Christian teaching about a Creator God and the importance of people living together in peace. How then could they object? He also observed that the Muslim pupils were more familiar with the *Qur'an* than the non-Muslims were with the Bible."

"Fair enough," observed Richard, "but I have some sympathy with the SU and I think you need to be a bit careful here, Dad. This is a Christian country; you are a minister of the national church. By all means treat people of other faiths with courtesy and respect but is there not a danger of undermining Christian integrity by appearing to regard it as just another option on some values and lifestyle menu?"

"I think Richard has a point," added Alison.

"Interfaith dialogue isn't really on the agenda in our village, but that's probably because the community is pretty homogeneous and monochrome. Apart from a couple of Jewish families most people would claim to be Christian with varying degrees of commitment, or agnostic. There's also a sense that Islam represents terrorism, harsh sharia law, subjugation of women, arranged marriages – all things that the Church should be speaking out against strongly. Surely, Luke, what people like you should be doing is working to strengthen the Church's witness, not dilute it. I'm sorry if that sounds harsh but I'm sure that's what a lot of people will think. And a lot of church folk think they are the ones being discriminated against – like that woman forbidden to wear a small cross at work and the registrar sacked for not being willing to conduct civil partnership ceremonies. Yet all sorts of concessions are made to people of minority faiths."

"I think that's a bit unfair," said Archie. "Frankly when you read about the real persecution suffered by Christians in countries like Pakistan it's nonsense, and an insult to their suffering, to talk of Christian persecution here. We are entirely free to go to church, distribute Bibles and run Christian outreach projects in our communities. Every four years there is a 'kirking' service in St Giles' Cathedral for the Scottish Parliament and south of the border twenty-six bishops of the Church of England sit in the House of Lords as members of the United Kingdom legislature. That doesn't sound like 'persecution' or even 'negative discrimination'.

But what we can't do – and rightly in my view – is assert a right to practice our faith in a way which denies other people <u>their</u> rights and freedoms. I happen to agree that it was nonsense not to let that airline check-in clerk wear a small cross and I would be equally supportive of allowing a Muslim woman in that position to wear a headscarf or a Sikh man to wear a turban. I'm not so sure about the registrar, though. Under the law of the land gay couples are entitled to enter a civil partnership and it is the registrar's job to give effect to that law."

"Yes," said Anne. (Was this turning into a sibling argument supported by their spouses?).

"I also think you're being a bit hard on Dad, Alison. OK, so you live in a mono-cultural community, but that is not the case for many people in this country. And it's not the case in many parts of the world either. Mercifully we do not live with the kind of terror visited on the streets of Iraq and Afghanistan, Jerusalem and Gaza but the consequences of that terror play out here and in other western countries. It's very easy to demonise all Muslims after events like 9/11 and that has consequences for community relations in Glasgow and Edinburgh. Dad can speak for himself, Richard, but I think that, far from undermining Christian integrity by making friends with Muslims, Jews, Sikhs and others, he is demonstrating that integrity. Are we not supposed to show love for God and our neighbour on the basis that our neighbour isn't just the person like us next door?"

"Thanks for acknowledging that I can speak for myself," said Luke, finally managing to get a word in edgeways."

"Perhaps it would reassure Richard and Alison if I said a little about the Christian element in the pilgrimage, which was really very strong. The group included people from the Church of Scotland, Roman Catholic and Anglican Churches and the Salvation Army. We stayed in Church of Scotland accommodation and we visited Christian sites in Jerusalem, Bethlehem and Galilee. I acted as tour guide for these sites and had every opportunity to speak on their significance. One of the first things that struck me was the sense of reverence with which everyone approached the visits."

"When we went to the Mount of Beatitudes overlooking the Sea of Galilee we paused, not just to admire the marvellous view, but to allow me to read the Beatitudes from the Sermon on the Mount and to talk briefly about Jesus' ministry in nearby places like Capernaum. Personally, I found that a very moving experience and afterwards a number of people from other faiths said they had too. In fact some picked up particularly on the saying, 'Blessed are the peacemakers', seeing it as an encapsulation of the whole purpose of the pilgrimage. OK, so I wasn't telling my fellow pilgrims to abandon their 'false religions' and embrace the Christian faith; but I was commending the Gospel to them in a way which enabled them to respond positively. Indeed in the days that followed we often returned to the theme of peace-making in our discussions, sharing the prominence given to peace and wholeness of being in all our religions."

"Another special moment was when I led the group on a walk down the Mount of Olives and we stopped at the lovely church known as *Dominus Flevit*. That means 'the Lord wept'. It's designed in the shape of a tear drop and it looks across to the old city - to the Western Wall, so sacred to Jews, and the Dome of the Rock, so sacred to Muslims. There we stood as I told the story of Jesus weeping over the city where he was shortly to be crucified; then the Jews and Muslims spoke of the significance of their holy places. It was a very special moment and the predominant sense was of sharing, not competing."

"So what happens now?" asked Richard.

"Well," replied Luke, "we are having a meeting of the group in a few weeks' time to reflect on the whole experience and work out ways in which we can share it with our own communities. Right from the start we decided that practical outcomes from the pilgrimage would be seen here in Scotland, as doors were opened and barriers broken down. So that's the strategy and, perhaps, in a year or two others might follow our lead and organise another pilgrimage. For example, a Sikh member of the group floated the idea of an interfaith pilgrimage to the Golden Temple at Amritsar."

"Well count me in on that one too," said Joyce in what Luke, Anne and Richard immediately recognised as her bringing people back to earth tone.

"But, it's getting late," she continued. "No doubt Katie and Marcus will be awake at the crack of dawn and we've got a full day tomorrow. Coffee and 'Cocoa Black' chocolates in the lounge and then I'm off to bed."

9

Fast forward to February 2012:

This decade of rich and varied interfaith memories came flooding back as Luke sat in his study on the morning of Thursday 2nd February 2012, reading about the row over an Aberdeen minister allowing a group of Hindus to worship in his church hall. Luke had always paid attention to times and seasons and observed to Joyce over breakfast that it was Candlemas Day, forty days after Christmas, when the Church remembered the presentation of the infant Jesus in the temple at Jerusalem.

"I'm sure the good folk of Capelaw will be talking of little else," Joyce had observed as she emptied the dishwasher. But then, softening, she entered into the spirit of the conversation, recalling an old rhyme about Candlemas Day and the duration of the winter.

"How does it go, again? Yes – something like this:
If Candlemas day be dry and fair
The half o' winters to come and mair
If Candlemas day be wet and foul
The half o' winter's gane at Yule."

"Well remembered," responded Luke. "It's a bit like the St. Swithin's Day rhyme about raining or not raining for forty days. Well let's hope it's wet and foul today to keep the winter short."

Now in his study and thinking towards the approaching Sunday the Candlemas theme of light shining in darkness stayed with him. He read the passage from Luke chapter 2, the *Nunc Dimittis,* and pondered again the words of Simeon which he had learned as a boy in the King James Version of the Bible:

> *Lord, now lettest thou thy servant depart in peace, according to thy word. For mine eyes have seen thy salvation which thou hast prepared before the face of all people; to be a light to lighten the Gentiles and to be the glory of thy people Israel.*

Luke loved the way his Evangelist namesake used song in his telling of the Christmas story. In chapter 1 Zechariah, the father of John the Baptist breaks into song with the *Benedictus – Blessed be the Lord God of Israel for he has visited and redeemed his people.* Then it is Mary's turn with the *Magnificat,* after Gabriel appears to her: *My soul doth magnify the Lord and my spirit hath rejoiced in God my Saviour.* Next come the angels of Bethlehem: *Glory to God in the highest, on earth peace, good will towards men.* Then we hear the final song of the quartet, the *Nunc Dimittis,* from the mouth of aged Simeon.

While a minor festival compared with Christmas and Easter, the Candlemas theme of light went to the heart, not just of Christianity, but of many religions. The controversy over the Hindus in the Church hall made Luke think of Diwali – a Hindu festival that focusses on light. And just a few weeks ago, he thought, as Christians celebrated Christmas Jews had their festival of Hanukkah. Indeed over Christmas Luke had noted an increasing number of menorah candles on window sills in homes he knew not to be Jewish. How ecumenical, but also how ironic that, with such a shared emphasis on light, the popular perception should be that religion was something for the unenlightened.

Thinking back to the interfaith pilgrimage four years ago Luke had to acknowledge that the follow-up had been less than intense. A de-briefing had taken place a few weeks after the return home. It had been good to see everyone again but even by then people had settled back into their old routines and the 'buzz' which had pervaded the group during their time in the Holy Land had largely gone. Some had already reported back to their own communities, where they had been heard with interest. There had been disappointment with a post-pilgrimage television interview with leaders of the group. The programme organisers had found an arch-cynic who poured scorn on the whole project, just stopping short of referring to the participants as useful idiots. Faced with such an onslaught it was difficult not to come across as defensive, but all agreed that this merely served to underline the importance of trying to live out ideals and values in an increasingly cynical world.

As with the earlier Syria trip Luke had given an account of his involvement to his kirk session and made reference to it in a Sunday sermon. He was also asked to speak to his presbytery where he was listened to politely, but the absence of any questions confirmed his feeling that 'politeness' was the appropriate word rather than 'interest'. More interest was evident when he had been invited by an Edinburgh rabbi, who had taken part in the pilgrimage, to share a platform at his synagogue. There had been some real engagement there, with lots of questions, some sympathetic, others verging on the hostile. But that was all right. It showed interest and a willingness to engage.

In his study that Candlemas morning Luke read the *Scotsman* report again, noting that the presbytery had refused to ban the Hindus from using the church hall for their twice monthly worship gathering. He had a sense, though, that this would not be the end of the matter.

"You watch" he had remarked to Joyce later in the day. "This will come up at the General Assembly in May."

It also dawned on him that this was the challenge for which he had been waiting. Here was an opportunity to re-engage with the interfaith process which had been rather side-lined by the 'gay clergy' controversy of the past few years.

This resolve was confirmed when, the following day, Luke took a phone call from Moira Paterson, a member of his congregation and President of the Guild. This was the new abbreviated name, reflecting gender inclusiveness, given to what was still widely known as the *Woman's Guild*. Luke had considerable respect for the organisation. His experience in all three of his parishes was that Guild members were often amongst the best informed and most committed members of the congregation – raising funds for good causes, attracting a range of excellent speakers to their meetings and, through their national organisation, engaging with government on a range of issues affecting social policy. In recent years, for example the Guild had taken a strong lead on subjects such as human trafficking, domestic abuse, prostitution and HIV-AIDS awareness. A caricature, equivalent to the *Women's Institute's* 'Jam and Jerusalem' image might linger, but Luke was scornful of such patronisation.

Moira was a serious and thoughtful woman and had been elected President of the Capelaw Guild branch two years previously. She had recently taken early retirement from a civil service role with the Scottish Parliament, and there was no doubt that the contacts and connections she had built up over the years, together with her persuasive charm, had resulted in a succession of top quality speakers making their way to Capelaw to address increasingly well attended meetings.

"Good morning, Luke," she began brightly.

Why is it, Luke wondered, that whenever Moira comes on the phone I suddenly find myself sitting up straight?

Out loud he responded: "Good morning to you too, Moira; always good to hear from you. I hope you are well."

"Perfectly, thank you," replied Moira, "and I trust you are too."

"I'm calling to ask if I might pop round sometime in the next few days. I was reading a piece in the *Scotsman* yesterday about that minister who's being given a hard time by some of his colleagues for allowing a group of Hindus to use his church hall for worship, and it's prompted me to get in touch. I've been thinking for some time that, maybe, the Guild could focus somehow on interfaith issues. I know this is an interest of yours," she continued, "and would value your thoughts."

"Interesting that you should mention this," replied Luke. "I've been thinking about this too. As you indicate, I've had quite a bit of involvement with interfaith work over recent years and recognise that there are those within the church who are uncertain about it. As it happens the diary is fairly light this week. How about coming around for a coffee tomorrow morning and we can have a chat."

This arrangement was quickly agreed and next morning Moira duly arrived at the manse.

After pleasantries and the serving of coffee the conversation began with Moira explaining how she continued to keep in touch with a number of former colleagues. One of these was a Muslim woman, Nadine, who had worked in the Scottish Government's equalities unit. A few days previously she and Nadine had met up for lunch and the conversation had turned to the way religion so often appeared to lie at the root of political and ethnic tensions around the world. They had also reflected on how an anti-immigrant narrative was developing, perhaps more so south of the border, but fully covered in UK-wide media with anti-Europe and anti-human rights agendas. Nadine had asked if Moira had any idea how unsettling this was to decent, hard-working, tax-paying, law-abiding members of minority communities, many of whom had been born in this country and knew no other home. After a leisurely lunch they had agreed to contact some church and mosque friends with a view to gathering a group of women for a conversation about what was going on.

"Both Nadine and I suspect that the members of such a group will find they have a great deal in common," she observed.

"One of the reasons I wanted to share this with you," Moira continued, "is that I'm wondering whether I might involve the Guild in the project. OK – so I get one or two people together, people I'll know will be sympathetic, and we'll meet with Nadine and her friends. But already I'm thinking ahead and asking myself – what next? And then I thought – wouldn't it be good to invite the Muslim women to a Guild meeting here in Capelaw? Nadine and I could each say something about the background to the initiative and then there would be an opportunity for the women to mix and converse. What do you think, Luke? Is this a crazy idea? How would the kirk session and the congregation react? I know we have one or two families with sons in the army in Afghanistan."

"I don't think it's crazy at all," said Luke, adding with a smile, "though I am reminded of a *Yes Minister* episode where Jim Hacker outlines a plan to Sir Humphrey who replies: 'That's a very courageous proposal, Minister.' This response immediately sends the politically risk-averse Jim into a panic."

"But seriously," Luke continued, "it's a great idea, but one to be managed carefully. I remember a few years ago when I shared something of my visit to Syria with the kirk session there were those who were rather negative about the whole thing. They approved of showing solidarity with the Syrian Christians but some didn't react so well to dialogue with Muslims. The phrase 'fraternising with the enemy' wasn't quite used but it felt like part of the sub-text. On the other hand there were those who did feel it was important for people of different faiths and cultures to meet and learn about traditions other than their own. Maggie Russell and Jean Thompson are both in the Guild, aren't they? They'd be very supportive and Maggie's well placed in her flower shop to pick up any grumbling and perhaps even counter it."

"That's a good thought," said Moira. "Clearly, if I pursue this idea I will need to take the Guild committee with me and Maggie's on the committee. I might even sound her out quietly. Jean attends the Guild, so it's good to know she'd be on board too."

"Do you want me to flag this up to the kirk session?" asked Luke. It was one of his disappointments that Moira had declined an invitation to become an elder. She had felt it wasn't really 'her thing' and that she could do her bit in other ways.

"I wouldn't say anything yet," was Moira's cautious response. "I'll speak to Maggie and Jean and perhaps they will agree to be part of my small team to meet with Nadine and her pals. I'll let you know how that goes and then we can take it from there – or not, as the case may be," she added with a shrug. "But nothing ventured . . ."

"Fine," said Luke. "We'll leave it at that."

And so the conversation turned to more general matters until Moira announced that she needed to be getting on.

"Thanks Luke," she said, giving him a parting peck on the cheek. "I really appreciate your support."

Later that day, over their evening meal, Luke told Joyce about Moira's ideas. She too approved.

"What an asset that woman is," was her assessment. We're lucky to have her and that's certainly a meeting I will go to."

Having started a young women's group in Luke's first parish and done a stint as Guild president in his second Joyce felt she had done her bit. To be fair to the Capelaw folk she had never come under any real pressure to lead the Guild, but she did try to attend meetings from time to time.

"You're quite fired up about this move to block the Hindus meeting in the church hall, aren't you?" she observed.

"I wouldn't put it quite like that," said Luke, somewhat peevishly. "But it's a straw in the wind indicative of a mind-set which feels that being too neighbourly to people of other faiths is somehow being untrue to our Christian heritage. I just can't accept that. Indeed, I think we would gain a lot of credibility as a national church if we took some kind of lead in the process of building bridges. Would that not be a good contribution to be making to our wider civil society?"

10

A couple of weeks later Luke received a letter from a friend who lived near Aberdeen. Knowing of his interest in interfaith matters he had sent him a copy of an article from his church magazine. The author, he explained, was a church member who had worked for a number of years in India and been a member of the Church of South India. She had recently been invited by an Indian friend to attend the *puja* (Hindu worship) in a church hall. This is what she wrote:

> When I arrived a lady and her young son took me inside and explained that most people sit on rugs laid out on the floor. There were a few chairs and it was suggested that I might be more comfortable on one of them! However, I chose to join a group of young women and children sitting together on one of the rugs, and a young woman came to sit beside me. Once the puja began she whispered to me from time to time, explaining what was happening.
>
> While words were recited, music played and a bell rung the statue of the God was washed, clothed and fed, symbolising the welcome we should give to God in our life and worship. Just as we offer these signs of welcome to guests who enter our homes so should we welcome God in our midst.

In the next part we sang several bhajans. These short worship songs are sung line by line: a small group sings each phrase which is then repeated by the whole congregation. I was able to join in singing these bhajans being familiar with this style of music from Christian worship in India. Many churches sing both hymns and bhajans during Sunday worship.

Towards the end of the puja we were invited to come forward to the priest to receive God's blessing for ourselves and our families. Food that had been brought was also blessed while two or three people sang and music was played. Worship then continued informally in the adjacent hall as we talked and shared in eating the Prasad (blessed food) together.

The whole afternoon was a wonderful experience. But what I will remember most is the wonderful welcome I was given.

As he read this article Luke thought of a story from the Old Testament, found in the Second Book of Kings, chapter 5. It concerns a man called Naaman who was a commander in the army of the King of Aram, an enemy of Israel. On one of their raids the Arameans had taken captive a young Hebrew girl who had ended up as a maid to Naaman's wife. Now, for all his military power and authority, Naaman was a leper and one day his wife's maid suggested that he seek a cure from the prophet Elisha. In time this indeed happened as, on the instructions of the prophet, Naaman washed himself seven times in the River Jordan. His healing led to an immediate religious conversion and submission to the God of Israel.

But this gave Naaman another problem on which he sought Elisha's opinion. From time to time Naaman would be expected to accompany his master and conform to the ritual when the King of Aram went to worship and sacrifice to his god in the House of Rimmon. Would this not now compromise his new found faith in the God of Israel? Would the God of Israel understand and forgive? Elisha's answer was short and to the point: "Go in peace."

As Luke had prayed in his Christian way in the Abu Nour Mosque in Damascus and in the Great Synagogue of Jerusalem, so could not this Christian writer of the article he had just read not similarly pray and graciously accept a blessing sincerely offered by a Hindu priest? Was any great damage being done that day to a church hall in Aberdeen by devout people of a visiting faith mingling their prayers with those of the host community? Luke thought too of another Old Testament story – again from the Books of Kings. When the great King Solomon built his temple in Jerusalem he offered this prayer: "But will God indeed dwell on the earth? Even heaven and the highest heaven cannot contain you, much less this house that I have built?" (1 Kings 8: 27).

That evening he showed the article to Joyce. Her initial thought had been to say, 'O you're not still on about the Hindus worshipping in the church hall, are you?'

Was her husband becoming more terrier-like as he got older? When does an interest start to become an obsession? Such thoughts crossed her mind, but what she said was:

"Yes, it's a good piece and clearly the writer's minister was quite relaxed about one of his members sitting in on a Hindu *puja,* else it might not have appeared in the church magazine."

"Do you know," she continued, gradually feeling less grumpy about Luke's 'obsession'. After all, how was he to know that what she had really wanted to discuss when they sat down that evening was a suitable present for their granddaughter's birthday which was just a couple of weeks away.

"Do you know," Joyce remarked, "the article reminds me of the MacLean wedding. Do you remember that?"

"Remember it, said Luke. "How could I forget? That was an exercise in diplomacy if ever there was one."

The MacLean wedding had involved a young man in Luke's previous church called Angus MacLean. His parents were members of the congregation and Angus and his brothers had gone through Sunday School, Bible Class and Youth Fellowship there. Angus had gone to university to study medicine and there he met Rawinder, also training to be a doctor. The relationship blossomed and on graduating they became engaged to be married. Rawinder's family was Sikh and when the time came to plan a wedding both she and Angus were agreed on wanting a religious ceremony. But which religion – Sikh or Christian? Some of their friends suggested they avoid the issue altogether and opt for a civil ceremony at the registrar's office. But neither favoured that choice – nor did their families. So they came to talk to Luke who had known Angus since he was a small boy in the primary Sunday School.

Over the years Luke had taken part in the occasional 'mixed marriage' ceremony, a term which normally signified a Catholic-Protestant union. It was quite difficult to recall, Luke realised, that once this had actually been quite a big deal. Traditionally the service would be held in the bride's church, with the host cleric presiding and the other assisting. But at least these marriages were Christian ceremonies allowing for a relatively straightforward blending of traditions. A Christian-Sikh marriage was of an entirely different order.

As Luke talked this through with Rawinder and Angus it soon became apparent that a single ceremony was a non-starter and would do justice to neither faith tradition. Indeed it would serve only to compromise both religions. The solution, therefore, which was soon reached, was that the blessing of both faiths should be invoked in separate but related ceremonies. This way both bride and groom could signal respect for the other's faith, something which was important to them. What impressed Luke was how much each had learned of the other's beliefs and how, in particular, Rawinder knew so many Christian hymns, gleaned from school assemblies. Luke indicated that he would be happy to co-operate. Meanwhile Rawinder said that she would talk to her parents and the Sikh authorities at their temple.

They too were co-operative with the result that when the day came a morning ceremony, with prayers and blessings, was held at the Sikh temple. This was followed by a lunch there, hosted by the bride's family, after which everyone made their way to the church. There a Christian marriage service took place, including the traditional wedding vows and the signing of the legal marriage schedule.

"Yes, it was quite a day," recalled Joyce. "How well the two families mixed – and weren't Rawinder's father and brothers resplendent in their tartan turbans."

"I'd forgotten that detail," smiled Luke. "But yes, it was a good day and a model of how respect can triumph over mistrust. And then a couple of years later, as I recall, a little boy was born and the question of a blessing arose," mused Luke. "That also called for some creative thinking, as I recall."

"Yes, I remember," said Joyce.

"The MacLeans hosted a ceremony in their home where you blessed the child. After that the Sikh grandfather offered prayers and gave a little homily on what the birth of a child meant within Sikhism, stressing parental duties and the care of the wider community. Then, as at the wedding, we all shared a meal."

"That little boy will be in his teens now. Do you have any contact with them?" asked Joyce.

"No," replied Luke," not since we moved here." But I must share the story with Moira when she gets back to me. I can't wait to hear how she gets on."

In the event Luke had to wait a few more weeks before he heard further from Moira. When she did get in touch it was to say that she had spoken to Maggie and Jean and both were 'up for it'. A date had still to be worked out with Nadine but she, too, had lined up some friends from the mosque. Moira was pressing for a get-together quite soon so that, if things went well, there would be time to factor something into the programme for the following Guild session.

Reassuringly for Joyce, still concerned about her husband's tendency to obsess, Luke's attention was soon taken up with other matters. Spring was a busy period in the parish year. Luke had established a Lenten Bible study series which was well attended. Holy Week and Easter services called for preparation and delivery. Capelaw Primary School looked to the parish minister as school chaplain to host an end of term Easter service, something Luke was always pleased to provide. Capelaw was a compact community with church and school very much at the heart of village life. In no time at all, it seemed, May had come around and for the Church of Scotland that means General Assembly time.

Luke wasn't a member of the 2012 Assembly, but finding himself in Edinburgh one day he decided to slip into the public gallery to see what was going on. Under consideration was the report of the Legal Questions Committee. Not the most exciting thing I could have chosen, Luke grumbled, but then, on perusing the order paper, a notice of motion caught his eye. It asked the General Assembly to instruct the committee to prepare legislation 'which ensures that acts of worship within all church property is Christian worship, offered exclusively to the one God who is Father, Son and Holy Ghost.'

Was I right or was I right, said Luke to himself. Did I not say this would find its way on to the agenda of the General Assembly?

The mover of the motion was careful not to target any particular congregation or faith, arguing in favour of a general principle. Those who supported him spoke of the uniqueness of Christ as Saviour of the world and the Church's calling to 'baptise all nations.' To allow the worship of 'false gods' in a building dedicated to Christian witness, they maintained, would amount to blasphemy and desecration.

Those who spoke against a ban focussed on grace and hospitality as appropriate expressions of Christian witness. They suggested that the message given by the proposed ban could be interpreted as the Church retreating into its own comfort zone, rather than engaging respectfully with people of another faith tradition. It was also strongly argued that decisions of this sort should be left to individual congregations who would have all the relevant local information.

At the end of the day the Assembly rejected the idea of a ban, though the vote was close, with 253 in favour and 289 against.

While dismissing this particular proposal the Assembly did go on to instruct a general review. This was on the successful motion of a youth delegate that 'a substantial report on all aspects of interfaith work, with particular reference to the place and practice of Christian mission in a multi-faith society', should be prepared and presented to the General Assembly of 2014.

"I told you the Hindu worship matter would come up at the General Assembly."

This was Luke to Joyce that evening, back at Capelaw Manse.

"So what happened?" asked Joyce. "Is the Assembly sending in the storm troopers to evict them? That'll make a good story for the media and show the Kirk in a really good light."

"No need for sarcasm," replied Luke, defensively.

"For your information, a banning move was thwarted, though the vote was close and our whole approach to interfaith matters is to be looked at over the next couple of years. Perhaps I'd better let Moira know she shouldn't hang about if she wants to proceed with her plan to invite the Muslim women to a Guild meeting."

"Surely that wouldn't create any waves," said Joyce.

"Perhaps not," agreed Luke, "though the return leg might."

11

In fact it was not long until Luke heard back from Moira.

The week following the General Assembly she phoned to ask if she could call round at the manse for a follow-up chat.

"I see there was an attempt at the Assembly to deny other faith groups access to church premises," she began."

"Yes indeed," responded Luke, "though, to be fair, the point of concern was worshipping as distinct from just meeting. I was there. Popped into the public gallery to see what was going on; noticed this banning motion on the order paper so decided to wait and see what happened. It was quite a short debate because the Assembly had a lot of business but the proposal didn't succeed. The vote was quite close though, which shows pretty clearly how divided opinion is. Maybe this is going to be the next hot topic after gay ministers!"

"I don't know about that," said Moira, "but I did notice that wasn't the end of the matter. I gather there is to be some kind of review of interfaith policy. I also just learned that the Church's interfaith officer has moved on and so far has not been replaced. Do you know what's happening there?"

"No I don't," replied Luke. "It may just be that after five years they want to review the role, which is fair enough. But we won't go into all of that just now. Let's find a time which suits us both and continue the conversation then."

A few days later, at the appointed time, Moira arrived and the conversation continued.

She began by relating how she, Maggie and Jean had had an excellent evening with Nadine and two of her friends. At Nadine's suggestion they had met for a meal at the *Mosque Kitchen,* a popular Middle Eastern restaurant just behind Edinburgh's Central Mosque. It had been a relaxed and unhurried occasion with some serious talking, but also some excellent shared humour. It turned out that Jean had taught the daughters of one of the Muslim women whose name was Asma.

"You're not at all as fierce as my girls described you," Asma had observed to much amusement. Then it transpired that Nadine's other friend, Rashid, had a flower shop in Leith, right on the other side of Edinburgh from Capelaw, so no threat to Maggie. Needless to say the two florists soon had much to talk about."

"Do you know what struck us all quite early in the conversation?"

This was Moira to Luke.

"What struck us was that the primary reason for meeting was that we were different. Maggie, Jean and I are Christian; Nadine, Asma and Rashid are Muslim. So that makes us different – but how different? In fact what we soon discovered was that we're not that different at all. We are all women for a start; we all think of ourselves as Scottish; Maggie and Rashid are florists; Jean taught Asma's children; Nadine and I were work colleagues and continue to be friends. We also discovered that we all enjoyed the food at the *Mosque Kitchen.* Not a place Maggie, Jean or I had ever thought of visiting - but you don't need to be a Muslim to eat there and we'll certainly be back."

"So why is it that, when we have so much in common, the one thing which is different – religion – should be given such a defining prominence?"

"A very good question," observed Luke. "I remember how in the early years of my ministry the week of prayer for Christian unity was just becoming established. All the local denominations would share a service – usually on a bleak January day – and agree that we had so much more in common than there were areas of disagreement. As we were all Christian that was hardly surprising. But what happens now, when we add other religions to the mix? Inevitably there will be more disagreement, but the question I always ask myself is 'What about our sheer humanity. Can that not be a common starting point?' At the heart of our Christian faith is the belief that God became human in Jesus Christ. I remember one of our professors telling us divinity students: 'if you're going to practise divinity you must first learn to practise humanity.' I've never forgotten that, which is why I absolutely agree with you. Why should difference of religion – or sectarian difference within the same religion –have the power to cancel out our sheer common humanity?"

"Sorry Moira. That was a bit preachy but, as you can see, it's something I feel quite strongly about. But tell me what happens now. Are you still thinking of doing something with the Guild?"

"Please don't apologise, Luke. I'm with you on this and hope that in some small way we can challenge popular prejudices about people who are 'different'." As Moira spoke the last word she made little inverted commas with her fingers.

"But to answer your question," she continued, "Yes I would like to move things on now. The Guild committee is meeting next week and this is on the agenda. Nadine, Asma and Rashid are keen on the idea of some kind of get-together, as are Jean and Maggie, but we thought we would make a start in a low key way. The plan is that our Guild should host a meeting of our own members with visitors from Nadine's mosque. To get things going we would offer some refreshments, then Nadine and I would each say something about the role of women in the church and the mosque. Did you know, Luke, that there is a bit of a debate going on over whether women should have a role in mosque management committees? Does that sound familiar? We would hope that our presentations might lead to some questions. Maggie, Jean, Asma and Rashid will take the lead there. The one thing we haven't quite worked out is how to close the meeting. I had wondered about reading a few verses from the Bible and having Nadine read from the *Qur'an*; or we may just allow a few moments for private prayer before we go home."

"That all sounds good," commented Luke. "Can I just check if it is your plan to keep this as an all-female event? Other people might well be interested and I know that sometimes you have open meetings. After all, the Guild membership is now open to men as well as women."

"I've thought about that," replied Moira "and it's something we discussed. We don't have any male members anyway, but our feeling is that on this occasion it should be a gathering just for women. Gender issues are somewhat sensitive in Islam. Men and women don't worship together, for example, and if we had male church members came along that might be unsettling for some of the Muslim women. I just think we should tread cautiously. If this goes well it might lead to further contact. Indeed, it occurs to me that you might like to make contact with the imam of the mosque at some stage."

"That's a thought," said Luke, "but meantime I take your point and am happy with that. It's the sort of thing somebody might ask about so it's as well to be clear."

"So you'll take this to the committee next week?" continued Luke.

"Yes, that's the plan. Maggie is very much on board and I'm not anticipating any great opposition – but it's certainly something different. What about the kirk session, though?" asked Moira, slightly anxiously."

"Well there's a meeting in a couple of weeks. You take your decision next week and, if it's a goer I'll inform the session as a matter of courtesy. There may be some questions but Maggie and Jean will be able to answer them and I'm sure it will all be fine."

Inevitably, there were questions at both meetings. One or two of the Guild ladies weren't sure about someone reading from the *Qur'an* in a church hall and wondered if the presbytery might need to give permission. Heaven forbid, thought Moira. They'd probably set up a committee and refer it to 121 George Street and we'd still be waiting for an answer in five years' time.

That's what she thought. What she said was that she had outlined her ideas to the minister. His response had been encouraging and, if the committee decided to go ahead, he would inform the kirk session. Any question of consulting the presbytery would be for them.

Another committee member asked about food. She'd heard people talking about *halal* food but didn't really know what that meant. Someone else thought that just had to do with meat, so probably wouldn't be an issue unless the plan was to serve a full meal. Moira agreed that getting the hospitality right would be important but the detail was something to be looked at in due course.

Someone else wondered if the Muslim women would be wearing western dress, or would some of them be veiled.

Maggie advised that that wasn't really something which had been discussed and wondered, with a touch of irritation, if that would be a problem. "Well, it would be nice to see their faces," someone muttered to her neighbour.

However, when eventually Moira asked for a decision on whether or not to go ahead such wariness was swept aside in a general enthusiasm for an initiative which, as someone put it, was 'new and imaginative'. At least she didn't say 'courageous', thought Moira, recalling Luke's *Yes Minister* story.

Later that evening Moira rang Luke to tell him how things had gone.

"So it's over to you and the kirk session now."

Capelaw being Capelaw the story was circulating the following day with the result that by the time the session met the following week it was really old news. The June meeting was usually a brief affair as summer holidays beckoned. There were reports on visits to the various church organisations with the usual appeals for more Sunday School teachers and singers, particularly men, for the choir. Bob MacEwan, retired local builder and active church property convener, also indicated that a couple of more volunteers to help with the church garden would also be useful. It occupied a prominent site on the main street and it was important that it looked 'cared for', as he put it.

It was this same gentleman who was on his feet again when Luke mentioned the proposal by the Guild committee to invite women from one of Edinburgh's mosques to a meeting.

"Is this something for the Guild committee to decide for itself?" Bob wondered.

"Well," responded Luke, "the Guild, like all the church organisations, comes under the authority of the kirk session and, recognising that this may be a bit controversial, Moira Paterson alerted me to the proposal and has asked that it be placed on the session's agenda this evening."

"But," continued Bob," is this not be something on which we ourselves should seek approval from the presbytery?"

Bob was also the kirk sessions' representative on the presbytery.

He continued: "It's quite a big thing to open our doors to Muslims and I hear there's even a suggestion that the meeting should include readings from the *Qur'an* – at a Christian church!" he added for emphasis.

A suspicion of Luke's was correct. Moira, as ever had been the soul of discretion but when she had mentioned someone on the committee asking about the presbytery he suspected it might have been Betty MacEwan, Bob's wife.

"If you're asking me for a ruling on the matter Bob," replied Luke, "then I would say the matter lies entirely within the competence of the session. I don't deny that the proposal is innovative for Capelaw, but over the past ten years since 9/11 the Church of Scotland has been encouraging interfaith engagement. In fact a report to last month's General Assembly stated that a recent poll showed that 85% of congregations thought interfaith work was important. Last December a Christian-Muslim Youth Conference was held and two years ago, in 2010, a Muslim speaker addressed the General Assembly for the first time. And, as you probably read, only last month the Assembly declined to pass a banning order on other faith groups meeting on church premises with the permission of local kirk sessions." (Luke believed in doing his homework.)

"OK, I accept that it's for us to consider, but I still think we should be careful. With Redford, Dreghorn and Glencorse Barracks all on the south side of Edinburgh we have a lot of army families in the area. And with Iraq and Afghanistan never out of the news Muslims aren't exactly the flavour of the month. Maybe that's a bit blunt but I've always believed in straight speaking and I'm just concerned that maybe here the Guild is asking for trouble."

"Let me say something," rejoined Jean Thompson. "I'm on the Guild committee and I can assure Bob that we are aware of sensitivities. Let's not get into the rights and wrongs of Iraq and Afghanistan, but we're living in Scotland in 2012. In a couple of years we'll be asked to vote in a referendum which will have huge implications for our children and grandchildren and the rest of the United Kingdom. Christians, Jews, Muslims, Sikhs, Hindus, Buddhists, Baha'is and people of no religious affiliation will be voting on the question of independence. As Scottish men and women we have a huge amount in common. Why should religion then be a cause of such division and suspicion?"

"Well said, Jean". This was Neil Jeffrey, a heating engineer with Scottish Gas and not one for speaking at every meeting on every item of business. This meant his occasional utterances tended to carry some weight.

"I have work colleagues who come from a variety of backgrounds but we all get along together. OK, if we're on a training course the Muslims probably won't come to the pub and the Sikhs are pretty distinctive in their turbans but, at the end of the day, we're all heating engineers upgrading our skills. I think this is a great idea and hope the session will give its full support to the Guild. In fact I hope it may lead to further opportunities for learning about cultures other than our own."

"Any other thoughts?" asked Luke.

"Like Jean, I'm a member of the Guild committee," said Maggie Russell. Can I just say that I hear the concerns which Bob is expressing and I've heard them too from customers. But sometimes we've got to move forward and this seems quite a small step. I remember one of the readings in the service last Sunday saying something about the ministry of reconciliation and surely that's more important than just isolating ourselves in our various comfort zones. It's not as if we're inviting an imam to preach the sermon next Sunday," she added to smiles. "Jean and I, along with Moira Paterson have met with three delightful ladies from the mosque. They're taking risks too and their people have similar issues to do with Iraq and Afghanistan – but from a different perspective. I hope, therefore, that the kirk session will give us its blessing."

As no-one else seemed minded to speak Brian MacFarlane, the session clerk, proposed that the elders express their support of the Guild's interfaith initiative and wish it every success.

"Is that agreed?" asked Luke. An approving rumbling of feet ensued, followed by Bob McEwan rising to say: "I'm content to have offered my opinion but I also respect the other views which have been expressed. I'm happy to go along with the decision so that the Guild can know it's unanimous."

This speech attracted an even louder rumbling, broken by Luke thanking Bob for his generosity of spirit and asking Maggie and Jean to convey the good wishes of the kirk session to the Guild.

12

The following morning the children from Capelaw Primary School came to church to mark the end of another school year. Such services were well established in the annual Capelaw cycle, as in similar communities across Scotland.

The Church of Scotland does not have its own schools but back in 1918, when public provision of separate Roman Catholic schools was agreed, there was a general assumption that the remaining state schools would retain some kind of connection with their local parish churches. This continued a historical link reflecting the priority given by John Knox and the sixteenth century reformers to having a school in every parish.

Over the course of the twentieth century such ties between church and school gradually loosened. Parish ministers continued to serve as school chaplains, albeit with the permission of the head teacher though, increasingly, this was no longer something to be assumed. In large secondary schools there might be a chaplaincy team, with a number of local clergy taking turns to conduct assemblies and end of term services. But the rise of religious and moral education as an examinable subject and the allocation of guidance responsibilities to professional teachers further undermined the chaplain's role as external provider of religious and pastoral input. Luke recalled one colleague remarking optimistically, as he tried to figure out the expectations of his school chaplaincy, that he supposed he was not so much the teacher as the visual aid.

A further challenge to traditional school chaplaincy came from the rising number of pupils from a background in other faith communities. In his Dundee ministry Luke had personal experience of this as a member of the chaplaincy team in a large secondary comprehensive. More recently he had had conversations on the subject with his daughter Anne. He recalled how at Joyce's' sixtieth birthday Anne had told how the chaplain in her school encouraged Muslim and Jewish pupils to contribute readings from their scriptures alongside the traditional Christian passages. Luke had taken a broadly similar approach but, looking back, he now wondered if such drawing of attention to these pupils created peer problems outside the assembly hall. In fact one of the things that had surprised Luke was how few parents from other faith backgrounds withdrew their children from religious assemblies. He reckoned it was in part because the children didn't wish that kind of attention to be drawn to them; but also in part because Muslims, Sikhs and others valued the fact that there was some religious input, even if it was not of their own tradition. He smiled as he remembered Rawinder and Angus and their Christian-Sikh wedding and Rawinder sharing how she had always enjoyed singing *Who would true valour see,* a favourite of her school's headmaster. Another of his favourites was *I feel the winds of God today, today my sail I lift,* probably, she added with a smile, reflecting the fact that he was a keen yachtsman. Luke noted that Bunyan had survived yet another hymnary revision but the winds of God had evidently blown themselves out.

Despite the social changes of the past century, in communities like Capelaw the old links endured and, provided he or she was not a total disaster, the minister was a generally welcome presence in the local school. Then, at the end of each term the pupils duly trooped along to the parish church to mark another milestone in their young lives. It was a good community occasion with parents and pre-school siblings also attending. Luke had provided readings and simple prayers and some of the older pupils had been selected and rehearsed to contribute these to the service. Quite often a group of pupils would stage a short presentation. This year the Primary 4 class acted out the parable of the Good Samaritan. Towards the end of the service a poignant moment arrived when the Head Teacher called the Primary 7s up, one by one, presented leaving certificates and wished them well on their move to the big school. From now on they would have to catch the school bus at 8.15 every morning and travel the eight miles to the county town where the secondary school was located. The service concluded with everyone singing Sidney Carter's popular hymn, *One more step along the world I go.*

A fair number of pupils (though not as many in former years) attended church and Sunday School and also participated enthusiastically in the church-run holiday club. A couple of the teachers and a classroom assistant were church members and this was a very helpful link. At the same time there were a number of pupils from other religions, including Muslim, Sikh and Hindu. None of these were ever excluded from school assemblies or services but their presence that morning, after the previous evening's session meeting, was felt keenly by Luke. What kind of Scotland would they be living in when they were his age, he wondered? Was there perhaps something to be said for the American pattern of complete separation between church and state in the educational sphere?

He recalled an American assistant coming to work with him for a year in his Dundee parish. The young man had greeted Luke with a cheery: "Hi, I'm John Randolph Spencer, but everyone calls me Randy."

Luke had responded by indicating that while in Scotland he would prefer him to go by the name 'John'. They had had a good laugh when Luke explained the reason.

But as well as overcoming the misunderstandings of a 'common language' there were also the social and cultural differences to negotiate. One of these had been John's utter astonishment at the prospect of a church minister going into a state school, effectively to promote the Christian Gospel. Luke reflected on the irony that, notwithstanding the fact that this would not happen in the States, church-going there seemed to be far stronger than in Scotland. He recalled an atheist friend telling how he sent his children to Sunday School to 'inoculate them against religion'. Was the decline in church attendance perhaps linked to an over feeding of religion to the young? But one thing which was clear was that the current bitter feuding between religious factions from Belfast to Baghdad was doing nothing but harm to the whole faith enterprise. No wonder a driving force in the recent 'Arab Spring' revolutions had been the demands of a younger generation for secular democracy in place of the old religious based dictatorships.

Such thoughts occupied Luke's mind as, after the school service, he made his away to Moira's house. He decided to call round on the chance that she was at home and report the outcome of the previous evening's session meeting. Moira lived on the edge of the village in what had originally been two farm cottages but which she and her late husband, John, had purchased and converted in anticipation of their retirement. Once the children had grown up and left home it was evident that the family home in Morningside was bigger than they needed. So it made sense to downsize and release some capital for their later years. It was not to be though – or at least not as planned. Just months after the move John, an Edinburgh solicitor, had died suddenly following a heart attack. Of course Moira was devastated, but in her stoical and practical way she took comfort from the fact that they had made the move together, so it wasn't something she had had to face on her own. She loved the new house, which was perfect for her needs, and while they had had good neighbours in Morningside, here in Capelaw she really felt part of a whole community.

"Good timing Luke," was her friendly greeting. "As you can see I've just been cutting the grass and was about to get myself a cold drink. Come and join me."

"Don't mind if I do," responded Luke. "You've done wonders with the garden, and the house. It was all quite dilapidated when we first came to Capelaw, but look at it now."

"Well it keeps me busy," said Moira "and I'm just so pleased John and I had those few months here. You know it's just coming up to three years since he died and finally I've got things more or less as we'd planned them.

In fact," she continued, "I was just thinking the other day that the first time John and I came to church after moving here you were talking about the interfaith pilgrimage to the Holy Land. We both thought it was fascinating."

"But enough of reminiscing," she added in a self-chiding tone. "Why don't we sit on the patio? Apple juice all right?"

It was a very pleasant Scottish June day with the temperature in the low twenties and the rain of the past week having finally moved on. There would be quite a bit of lawn mowing in Capelaw over the next day or two, Luke reckoned – not forgetting the manse garden.

"So how did things go at the kirk session?" asked Moira, once they were seated and after they had admired the fine uninterrupted view across fields to the Pentlands Hills. "I never tire of this view," Moira remarked, "whatever the weather, whatever the season."

Luke summarised the previous evening's discussion, at the same time studiously avoiding attribution of particular opinions to individual elders. That said, he suspected that Moira was sufficiently shrewd to match thoughts to people, though too tactful to give any such indication.

"Well that's good news, indeed - and here's to the occasion," she smiled, raising her glass "and appropriately toasted in nothing stronger than apple juice!"

"As time was getting on," she continued, "we already allocated a date in the syllabus to be confirmed once everyone had agreed. We thought earlier in the session would be best and certainly before winter if we're expecting people to come out from Edinburgh. The last Tuesday in September is the date we have in mind."

Luke remembered how back in the 1950s his mother's Woman's Guild met on a Tuesday evening – Ah, the laws of the Medes and the Persians, he thought!

"And here's another thing," continued Moira. "You remember I said maybe you should make contact with the imam at Nadine's mosque? Well I think you've already met him. Nadine thought she'd better have a word with him about what was being planned and mentioned your name. Apparently he was on the interfaith pilgrimage to the Holy Land you and Joyce went on a few years ago."

"You don't say," was Luke's response. "There were a couple of imams in the party but I'm sure they were both from Glasgow. What's his name?"

Moira couldn't recall off hand but said she'd get the information to Luke and he could follow it up.

So it came about that a few weeks later an arrangement was made for Luke himself to call at the mosque and renew his acquaintanceship with Imam Ubayd Malik who had indeed been based in Glasgow at the time of the pilgrimage, but had recently moved to one of the Edinburgh mosques. Over coffee and biscuits in the imam's office the two men had reminisced over their shared experience as members of such a diverse faith group travelling around Israel and Palestine. Imam Ubayd commented particularly on the warm welcome they had all felt when entering the Scottish guest-house at St Andrew's Church in Jerusalem. Like Luke he had some regrets that there had never been any real follow up, but acknowledged that was often the way with these things. People were busy living their own lives within their own families and communities and somehow time just passed and good intentions never got translated into deeds.

Somewhat anxiously Luke asked how Ubayd felt about the initiative which Nadine and Moira were following up. He need not have worried.

"It's a good and a fine thing the women are doing," he had replied. "We appreciate the invitation from your women's group and hope it will lead to better understanding. You know, we welcome visitors to the mosque and are happy to show people round. In fact we have had a number of school groups over the past few months. But all it takes is for a terrorist incident or a news report about some crazy hate preacher in a mosque and parents start withdrawing their children. People never seem to hear the Muslim condemnations of atrocities. We are not all fanatics, you know."

"I know that," said Luke, "but 'Muslims condemn attack' will never get as prominent a headline in the popular press as 'Prime Minister condemns Muslim fanatics'. But let's see how the September meeting with the women goes and then perhaps we can look at some follow up."

"Yes, let's do that," responded Ubayd. "Maybe we can have a return visit here - or perhaps you and I might work together on a public conversation which we could share at the mosque here and in your church. What do you think, Luke," he smiled, "a travelling road show?"

"OK," said Luke. "One step at a time but I might well be up for that. Let's keep in touch and we'll talk again later in the year."

13

That summer Luke and Joyce holidayed in Somerset where they rented a cottage near Bath. This provided them with a pleasant base from which to savour the charms of that city and explore the surrounding area from Lacock Abbey to Wells Cathedral.

"Do you remember bringing the children here when they were about nine or ten?" Joyce recalled. "They used to talk about 'mum's educational outings.' Poor wee things. What chance did they have with a teacher for a mother and a minister for a father?"

"Yes," laughed Luke, sharing the reminiscence. "And remember the holiday in Devon when we all went to choral evensong at Exeter Cathedral and caught Anne and Richard making faces at the choirboys during the sermon."

"Yes," said Joyce, "and I also remember the choirboys responding in kind. I wonder who really started it."

"And the time we brought them here to Bath to show them the Roman baths, Jane Austen's house and the Abbey. Afterwards we asked them what they had enjoyed most. Do you remember the answer?

"Yes, I do," said Luke – "burgers at the Wimpey!"

"Well they turned out all right," said Joyce. "Something clearly rubbed off."

The fortnight's holiday passed all too quickly and late August found them back in Capelaw with Luke gearing up for the start of a new church year. There was still sufficient breathing space, though, to take in some of the many options presented by the Edinburgh Festival, then in full swing, and its ever popular fringe. Luke and Joyce particularly enjoyed the Book Festival in Charlotte Square with the chance to hear a favourite author (if you were lucky enough to get a ticket) or just to soak up the atmosphere and mingle with visitors from around the world.

While Luke and Joyce were enjoying some free time Moira, Maggie and Jean had been beavering away, making arrangements for the special Guild meeting with their Muslim guests. This had generated quite a bit of interest with a report of the planned meeting even carried in the local newspaper. This had prompted one or two letters to the editor. Luke was reassured to note that these were generally supportive of the idea.

He was also pleased that, following the June session meeting, he had decided to let the presbytery clerk know what was afoot. In some respects the presbytery clerk is akin to a bishop, though without the formal authority which a real bishop has over the clergy. The Rev James Morrison had combined the clerkship with his ministry in a small rural parish and had continued in the role after his retirement. He was well respected by his colleagues and was invariably proactive in heading off trouble and in limiting damage. Luke, while he could be terrier-like when he got an idea into his head also had a canny streak and was a great believer in the principle that forewarned is forearmed. He had no doubt that the proposal to have a shared Guild meeting with Muslims was entirely for the Guild branch and kirk session to decide. At the same time he had judged it prudent to let the clerk know what was afoot. As he had put it to James, with a degree of prophecy: "I didn't want you reading about it in the local paper."

James was, as Luke had anticipated, quite relaxed.

"Good to see you Luke; come in and have a cup of coffee," had been his greeting, followed by "How's the parish? Have things settled down after last year's rumblings over the civil partnership blessing?"

"Oh, yes, that all seems to be in the past," said Luke, "and church life is back to normal. However, I just wanted to make you aware of something coming up which might reach your ears."

"My, my, Luke," smiled James, "I thought at your stage you'd be looking for a quiet life. Don't tell me you're still living dangerously. So what's going on?"

Luke told James about the planned Guild meeting and the discussion with the elders about it.

"That sounds like an excellent initiative. I agree it's entirely something for you and your people to decide, but I appreciate your letting me know."

James continued: "But clearly it's a sensitive issue for some and there are mixed messages out there. That business at the Assembly which we all know was about the Hindus using a church hall in Aberdeen; and now this review of interfaith policy over the next couple of years. Yet just two years ago we had Mona Siddiqui addressing the General Assembly and getting a very warm welcome. I don't think you were there that year, Luke, but if you haven't read it look at the report of the Youth Assembly. It's got a whole section on inter-faith matters. Let me show you."

James reached for the 2010 volume of Assembly reports.

Goodness, marvelled Luke, he's got reports going back to 1910 up there on his shelves!

"Look here," continued James, "the Youth Assembly is calling for 'education about all faiths to avoid stereo-typing based on media reporting'; and see here - 'encourage more practical support to congregations engaging in inter-faith relationships'; and look - a call for the Church of Scotland 'to recognise the values we share with other faiths'; and here - something about creating 'opportunities for people of other faith communities to speak to churches about their beliefs.'

"This is from the young people, Luke – the future of the Church! So I say, well done to your Guild ladies. I can't believe you'll get any grief over this but if I hear any muttering I'll let you know."

"Well thank you for that, James," responded Luke. "I'm glad I called and when I get back to the manse I'll fish out that 2010 Youth Assembly report. You're right. I wasn't at the Assembly that year, so much of what happened passed me by."

In the event the Guild meeting on the last Tuesday of September was voted a great success. Normally at such a special gathering the minister would have at least looked in to signify welcome and perhaps even say a few words. But, respecting the decision that this should be an exclusively female gathering, Luke stayed away. However, as she had indicated, Joyce was keen to attend and did so. When she arrived home Luke had the kettle on and was ready to hear her observations.

"Goodness, give me a minute to get my coat off."

These were her first words as Luke came bounding out into the hall as he heard her coming in the front door.

"How was it?" he had asked eagerly.

Once they were seated Joyce reassured her husband that it been 'an excellent occasion'.

"There were between forty and fifty there," she went on, "more or less evenly split between our Guild and the Muslim women. The hall had been set up with tables for eight. We were directed to tables so that we had four from each group, including a host from the Guild committee. There was water, fruit juice and nibbles and we were asked to introduce ourselves and help ourselves to refreshments."

"This settling down took about twenty minutes, by which time the ice was well and truly broken. Then Moira gave an excellent talk, welcoming everyone, and going on to say something about women in the Bible and the role of women in the church. After that Nadine spoke. She explained that the *Qur'an* stressed the equality of women and men and picked up on a point Moira had made about men and women being created alike in the image of God. Nadine then explained how in Islam the custom had developed of men and women worshipping separately, as is the custom in the Jewish synagogue. In fact, in the question and answer session later Jean Thompson made the point that after the Reformation men and women sat as separate groups in Church of Scotland services. I didn't know that."

"I think I remember reading that somewhere," interjected Luke. "But go on".

"Well there were quite a lot of questions – about dress, family life, prohibition of alcohol. Quite a few of the Muslim women were wearing head scarves and full length dresses while others wore western clothes. Interestingly, there seemed to be general agreement that there was something to be said for modesty in apparel, and that beach wear should be confined to the beach – for men as well as women! There were also harder questions about extremism and terrorism and Moira and Nadine handled these very sensitively. It was clear that the Muslim women had no time for the likes of the Taliban and the people responsible for 9/11. At the same time they had questions about Iraq and American drone attacks which killed civilians in Pakistan. They also bridled when they were made to feel like incomers or strangers when most of them had been born and brought up in the UK. At the same time they recognised how the families of soldiers in Afghanistan must feel when sons were killed or horribly injured by roadside bombs and the like. So there was some deep stuff going on. It wasn't just about clothes and recipes!"

"So did Moira and Nadine respond to the various questions?"

"Mostly, though others chipped in – like Jean talking about worship in the Reformation period. Then, after the questions tea, coffee and home baking was served and we chatted a bit more at our tables."

"So how did the meeting close?" asked Luke.

"Well, Nadine issued an invitation for another get-together, this time at the mosque and this was agreed enthusiastically. Then she read a few verses from the *Qur'an* which spoke of God as the light of heaven and earth and how we are guided to that light. It was beautiful. After that she said a Muslim prayer. It was very simple and I asked her if I could write it down – and not just because I thought you'd ask! Here's her prayer: 'It's glory enough for me that I should be Your servant; it is grace enough for me that You should be my Lord.'"

"Then Moira read the Bible passage about Jesus visiting the home of Mary and Martha, with its emphasis on practical service and devotional listening. Women do both, she stressed. She followed that with the famous prayer of Francis of Assisi – 'Lord make me an instrument of your peace'. You know," continued Joyce, "I remember learning that in school":

> *Lord make me an instrument of your peace.*
> *Where there is hatred, let me sow love,*
> *Where there is injury, pardon;*
> *Where there is doubt, faith;*
> *Where there is despair, hope;*
> *Where there is darkness, light;*
> *Where there is sadness, joy.*

"All in all, it was an excellent evening. We came away with a sense of having made new friends, but also with a lot to think about. By the way, Nadine said to pass on regards from Imam Ubayd. He hopes to meet up with you again soon. I also met his wife, Misha, though we didn't have much chance to talk. I wonder if being an imam's wife is anything like being a minister's wife," Joyce concluded with an impish smile.

"Yes, I'll get in touch with Ubayd once Nadine and her friends have had a chance to give him their take on the evening. Then he and I will need to think how we can build on what Moira and the Guild have started!"

The following week there was a kirk session meeting. As a courtesy Moira had been invited for the start of the meeting so that, along with Maggie and Jean, she could let the elders know how this first Capelaw interfaith occasion had gone. As quite a few of the Guild members were the wives of elders, who had no doubt undergone the same kind of interrogation as Joyce, this had the potential to be something of a formality. However, this was not the case. The same kind of questions came up as at the Guild meeting itself and the general tone of the discussion was warm and welcoming. So much of the business of a kirk session can seem routine and repetitive. It was as if the elders as a group were relishing the opportunity to have a fresh topic for discussion.

Riding the crest of this positive feeling Luke reported that he had had a conversation with the imam of the mosque who, as it happened, had been one of the Muslim representatives on his interfaith pilgrimage to the Holy Land four years earlier. He then outlined the tentative idea that he and Imam Ubayd might have a 'public conversation' outlining basic tenets of the two religions. Perhaps, he suggested, this might lead to some kind of meeting involving the session and the mosque management team.

"But let's just take things one step at a time," he added, reassuringly for some. "I will be meeting the imam in the next couple of weeks to gauge his reaction to the Guild meeting and will report on that to the session next month."

This was greeted with approving nods which developed into warm foot stamping as Luke thanked Moira and the Guild members for taking such a lead.

Reflecting afterwards with Joyce – and this time he allowed himself a modest celebratory dram – Luke remarked how both the gay clergy controversy and now the interfaith questions were stretching people to engage with matters beyond their comfort zones.

"Our faith," he began to preach to his congregation of one, "is a living faith and God is Holy Spirit as well as Father and Son. We are not just practitioners of an ancient code, set and settled once and for all. There are so many questions around – end of life issues, living wills, medical developments, not to mention political paralysis in face of climate change, world poverty, sectarian wars etc. etc. It's not just a case of rummaging through the Bible to find the answers to these questions. Yes there is wisdom there and principles for living a good life – but we need the fresh insights of the Spirit as we grapple day by day and I felt something of the Spirit moving in tonight's session meeting."

"That was quite a speech," responded Joyce.

"If you can remember it when you're writing your sermon in the morning I suspect I might hear it again on Sunday."

14

Over the course of the next few months two new interfaith developments caught Luke's attention.

The first of these was of a rather sombre nature. It concerned *A Gathering for Syria* to be held in Edinburgh's St Giles' Cathedral towards the end of October 2012. Luke had spotted a notice about this in the presbytery papers. At the same time the organisers, no doubt recalling his membership of the Moderator's delegation ten years previously, had sent a personal invitation to him and Joyce to attend. The letter from 121 George Street indicated that this would be an interfaith gathering and that it was being co-hosted by the Church of Scotland and the Edinburgh Interfaith Association.

The situation in Syria was indeed dire. Every day brought reports of fresh atrocities. The news litany of place names stirred warm and affectionate memories, but these quickly turned to dust with the ghastly television shots of carnage from Aleppo, Homs, Hama, Damascus. What, Luke wondered was this *Gathering for Syria* all about and what would it achieve?

So, on a dark October evening around Hallowe'en time, Luke and Joyce did take themselves into Edinburgh and joined a large and culturally diverse congregation. On previous visits to the Cathedral the pre-service music had comprised perhaps a Bach fugue or a Cesar Franck chorale played on the splendid Rieger organ, but not on this occasion. Instead, as people took their seats, the ancient stones reverberated to the Middle Eastern music of the Edinburgh based Dunya Ensemble.

Luke had heard on the grapevine that the event, though held in the Cathedral and comprising hymns and prayers, was not to be designated a 'service'. This was partly out of sensitivity to Christians who, while open to interfaith dialogue, had a problem with anything which might be construed as interfaith worship. At the same time the non-ecclesiastical title was respectful to those of other faiths (or none) who wished to express their solidarity with Syrians in their suffering.

Luke wondered how those contributing would approach the occasion. By now he had spotted individuals he recognised, including a couple of members of the Scottish Parliament, some city councillors, clergy from various denominations and people from different faith communities. In such a gathering those leading the proceedings would need to be sensitive, not only to a variety of beliefs, but also to the presence of non-belief. He recalled a story of a former Dean of St Paul's Cathedral in London who, presiding at civic service, announced a period of silence during which he invited believers to pray and free thinkers to think freely. Quite a nice line, thought Luke.

After words of welcome from the Minister of St Giles' the Moderator whom Luke had accompanied to Syria spoke and recalled the cordial interfaith atmosphere he had sensed during that visit a decade ago. He quoted William Dalrymple, whose book *From the Holy Mountain* so beautifully illustrated such connections, but who now expressed despair in what he described as 'the ripping apart of Syria's closely woven sectarian patchwork.' This ripping apart was later amplified in the reading of messages from the National Evangelical Synod of Syria and Lebanon and the Maronite Archbishop of Damascus. These spoke of the intensity of the violence and the huge number of innocent people killed as 'beyond description, or even imagination.' The archbishop's message contained a graphic account of a car bomb which only the previous week had shaken the Christian quarter of Bab Touma in Damascus, leaving thirteen dead and dozens injured. He concluded with a question and a plea: 'The Christian message is primarily that of the Cross of salvation, of love, of forgiveness. Will we have the courage to assume the prophetic adventure? Faced with this challenge, and in this chaotic and bitter loneliness, we need so much your prayers and your friendship.'

A few moments later there was a sound not normally heard in St Giles', though this was not the first time it had been heard. It was the Muslim Call to Prayer, intoned by a young Damascene architect living and working in Edinburgh, grateful to have work and sanctuary in Scotland, but fearful for his family still living in Damascus. He read from the *Qur'an* and stressed that 'like all other religions Islam promotes peace, love and harmony among people.' He reminded the gathering that the word 'Islam' is derived from the Arabic word *Salaam* which means 'peace', as does the almost identical Hebrew word *Shalom*. He told how the Prophet Muhammad had ordered his fellow Muslims to 'salute others, Muslims or non-Muslims, with peace' and how 'it is a rule in Islam that during war time an enemy warrior who pronounces peace is totally immune.'

Luke was also interested in the hymns chosen for the occasion. Clearly the organisers had judged it good to provide an opportunity for people to 'join in'. At the same time they had sought to be sensitive to the multi and non-faith nature of the gathering. Luke thought they had got it about right with *Immortal Invisible* at the beginning. He recalled his conversation with the Buddhist nun on Holy Island for whom this was a favourite, remembered from her early upbringing in the Church of Scotland. Its affirmation of a God who gives life and lives in all life felt appropriate. The closing hymn also seemed apt as it spoke of God's kingdom coming when 'justice shall be throned with might and every hurt be healed.' The reading of the Beatitudes with their reference to peacemakers also struck Luke as well-judged, reminding him of the interfaith pilgrimage to the Holy Land four years previously. Afterwards refreshments were provided for all and Luke and Joyce managed to speak to quite a few people from his years with the Interfaith Council. It was a good way to conclude the evening.

In the following weeks some criticism of the event did reach his ears. Some had felt there was too much emphasis on Syrian Christians suffering persecution, when in fact many Muslims were also suffering in the civil war. (Luke thought of the Aleppo Mufti's assassinated son.) Given the fact that the initiative was mainly church led, including contributions from Syrian churches, perhaps such an impression was inevitable. At the same time it also showed the difficulties inherent in trying to be inclusive and accommodate such diverse sensitivities.

The Gathering had been a sombre occasion but some months later, in March 2013, another interfaith development of an entirely different nature caught Luke's attention and captured his imagination.

A press report from Aberdeen told how the rector of a Scottish Episcopal Church in the city was offering hospitality to worshippers from a neighbouring mosque. What is it about Aberdeen, wondered Luke. One of our churches is giving a home to Hindus and now here is another denomination opening its doors to Muslims. Surely, he thought, if anywhere has a claim to be the interfaith capital of Scotland it is the Granite City whose heart is clearly made of softer material.

It was quite a touching story really.

On a bleak winter's day the rector noticed a number of Muslim men praying on the street. It was cold and wet, with swirling snow showers. What's going on, he wondered and his inquiries led to the discovery that the mosque was too small to accommodate the 200 or so Muslims who wished to attend Friday prayers. As a consequence the younger and fitter men offered to pray out of doors.

'Their hands and feet were bare and you could see their breath in the freezing cold,' the rector was reported as saying.

Since the mosque was close by the church, which was not used for Christian worship on a Friday, it occurred to the rector that the appropriate response would be to offer some neighbourly hospitality. Not everyone was happy but eventually his congregation agreed and, after some initial hesitation by the Muslims as well, that is what happened.

As he investigated further Luke learned that this was but a further step in a journey which had begun on Christmas Eve 2010. This fell on a Friday and prayers had been offered simultaneously in church and neighbouring mosque, after which the doors of both were opened and food provided for people in the neighbourhood. Then on the tenth anniversary of 9/11 a joint service had been held with readings from the Bible and the *Qur'an*. After the service the rector issued a statement which said: 'We had the sense that we were in this together and we really wanted to convey the message that, if we are genuinely seeking peace, we had to work together and pray together.'

In these sentiments the rector was supported by his bishop as, recalled Luke, the minister who granted the Hindus use of his church hall was supported by his presbytery. The Bishop of Aberdeen and Orkney was quoted as saying: 'Internationally, the news speaks of tension and struggles between Islam and Christianity. Yet, here in Aberdeen, a mosque and a church have built bonds of affection and friendship. It must be stressed that neither has surrendered or compromised any aspect of the historic faith to which each holds. But mutual hospitality and goodwill exists.'

Not everyone will see it that way, surmised Luke, and he was right. It wasn't long before follow up media stories reported on-line abuse coming the rector's way.

While Luke found the story touching he immediately spotted a difference between this case and the provision made for the Hindu congregation. The Hindus worshipped in the church hall, a space typically used for all sorts of community and recreational purposes – badminton, country dancing, youth organisations, coffee mornings, perhaps even as a polling station on election days. In other words, a church hall wouldn't have the same sense of sacred space as a church sanctuary, dedicated and set apart for Christian worship. Luke wasn't surprised, therefore, to read criticism which spoke of 'desecration' of the church by allowing Muslim prayer alongside a Christian altar and in the presence of powerful Christian symbols such as the Cross. No doubt, he thought, those within the church who were uncertain had similar anxieties. And, from the opposite point of view, he wondered whether the initial hesitation by the Muslims had been a concern about this, either from a perspective of not wishing to offend, or from a feeling that praying in the midst of such symbols would sully their own piety. He also sensed a distinction between people of different faiths coming together for an occasional act of shared devotion, as in the *Gathering for Syria,* and the making over of one religion's sacred space for the regular use of another. The critical question, he concluded, was whether genuine mutual respect remained or whether, as some of the more extreme on-line comment suggested, it was all part of an Islamic plot to take over the world.

By now Luke and Imam Ubayd had met on a couple of occasions with a further meeting planned for after Easter. That will give me a chance to ask what he thinks of the Aberdeen arrangement, Luke thought. The first meeting between the two men had been prior to the Guild get-together. It was on Moira Paterson's instigation but certainly Luke felt that he and Ubayd had 'hit it off', though he had to explain that the expression signified not aggression but harmony. They had met again, also at the mosque, at the beginning the Christian season of Advent. The idea was that Luke should say something about this season of preparation for Christmas. Then Ubayd would explain the significance of Ramadan, the Islamic holy month which had been observed earlier in the year. This way both men had something substantial to share; otherwise their meetings could end up being purely social.

In addition they still nurtured the idea of having a 'public conversation' and these one-on-one meetings offered some rehearsal space for this.

The post-Easter meeting, though, was to have a social dimension. Imam Ubayd and his wife, Misha were to come to the manse at Capelaw for morning coffee with Luke and Joyce. Misha had been with the women attending the shared Guild event the previous September and the two women had met briefly then. Joyce had wondered whether the role of an imam's wife would be anything like that of the 'traditional' minister's wife in Scottish culture. In any event that was all changing. The modern minister was as likely to have a husband and where the minister was male and married his wife was probably pursuing her own career. Joyce herself had lived through this period of transition. In the early years as a young mum she had started a young women's group in Glenburn. By the middle years she had gone back to teaching so was not around for daytime events in the parish. She had done a three year stint as president of the Guild at St Fillan's in Dundee, but as there was a good leadership team she was able to hand on that responsibility when her term was up. Now that she was retired she was content to be at home and had no objections to answering the phone and, within reason, giving time to chatty parishioners.

When the day came for the manse and mosque couples to meet it emerged that the two women had quite a bit in common. Misha did have her own career, as a doctor. She had chosen to go down the GP route and worked three days a week at a practice in the Gorgie area of Edinburgh. She and Ubayd were younger than Joyce and Luke and their two girls were still at school. The elder daughter hoped to follow her mother into medicine; the younger one had not yet set her heart on a career but, as she was just fifteen, there was plenty of time. Misha, it turned out, was also quite active in mosque affairs, organising a team of guides who welcomed visitor groups and provided hospitality. Whether it was a good opportunity for an outing or out of genuine interest, Misha remarked, the mosque was a popular venue for school groups and not just those specialising in religious studies. Numbers usually dropped after some terrorist incident, she had commented, mainly through parents withdrawing their children – but we understand that, she added and, hopefully, it's just temporary.

"But how are your plans for some kind of presentation coming along?"

This was Joyce to Ubayd.

"Well," he replied, looking tentatively at Luke, "we're getting there, I think. The two of us have had a couple of good conversations. The last one was about seasons. I explained Ramadan and Luke talked about Advent and Christmas. That was good and maybe there's a basis there for something more public."

"You know," said Luke, "I think we should just go for it. We're both pretty experienced. We know our stuff so why don't we plan a couple of 'gigs' (if that's not too irreverent a word) – one here and one at the mosque. I've already cleared the concept with my kirk session –equivalent I suppose to your mosque management committee – and they're fine with it. In fact, they're more than fine. Since the Guild meeting they are really quite keen".

"My thought," continued Luke, "is to make it an open meeting in the church hall here. We can seat a couple of hundred. We won't get anything like that but we could still get quite a crowd, and not just from the church. It's a bit ironic really. If I announced I was going to speak about Christianity at a public meeting I don't suppose many would turn up. They'd say 'we can go to church on Sunday any time we want.' But if I announce I'm going to have a conversation with an imam that might get people thinking and even coming along."

Ubayd smiled at this but said he was happy to proceed in this way. We need to take the leap of faith. "And then," he added, "we'll do the same at the mosque and make that an open meeting too, so men and women can come together."

"Well, it sounds like that's sorted," said Misha, "and if it's as good as that women's meeting here last autumn it will be well worthwhile.

Over coffee the conversation then turned to the Aberdeen story of Muslim prayers in the Church. Both Ubayd and Misha recognised the sensitivities involved, praising the rector and the bishop for their kindness but understanding those who were anxious that sacred principles should not be compromised.

"The big question," Ubayd continued, "is whether Muslims and Christians believe they worship the same God, albeit understanding God's nature in different ways. Perhaps *that's* something we can explore in our mosque and church conversations later in the year.'

15

While this Christian Muslim cordiality was underway between Luke and Ubayd and between the Aberdeen rector and the neighbouring mosque, tensions were emerging between the Church of Scotland and the Jewish community. These were created by a report prepared for the General Assembly in May 2013. Entitled *The Inheritance of Abraham? A Report on the 'promised land'*. The clue to the controversy lies in the question mark and inverted commas.

As originally published the report asked the General Assembly to refute claims that Scripture offered any peoples a privileged claim for possession of a particular territory. Against a background of settlement expansion this was contentious enough. However, the perceived offence was compounded by the lack of any acknowledgement of Israel's right to exist. In response to protests the authors met with members of the Jewish community, listened to their concerns and brought a revised text to the General Assembly. This affirmed the right of both Israel and a Palestinian State to exist in peace and security and was readily accepted. With regard to the specific Scriptural claims the Assembly conceded scope for argument, as distinct from outright rejection of the Jewish perspective, by deciding to 'dispute' rather than 'refute' the view that Scripture offers any peoples a privileged claim for possession of a particular territory – a subtle but significant amendment.

In the course of the debate a well-respected theologian reminded the General Assembly of a report from ten years previously which he had helped draw up. This had emphatically rejected the doctrine of 'supersessionism' which held that Christianity had superseded or replaced Judaism. He expressed the wish that the *Inheritance of Abraham* report had been a bit clearer on this point and reminded the Assembly that the Church of Scotland affirmed Judaism as a faith which continues to flourish under the providence of God. It was therefore not for Christians to instruct Jews on how they should read their own sacred texts. At the same time, such affirmation of Judaism as a continuing and flourishing faith did not preclude criticism of the modern state of Israel and its policies. Indeed, he suggested, the need for such criticism had intensified over recent years as a result of the location of the new security wall, the further expansion of Jewish settlements in the West Bank and the blockade of Gaza.

Luke had become aware of the brewing row and had, in fact, been contacted by some of his Jewish friends. He thought back to the interfaith Holy Land pilgrimage when, despite the *bonhomie*, tensions were never very far beneath the surface. For example, a Palestinian politician who addressed the group likened modern day Israel/Palestine to apartheid South Africa. This infuriated Jewish members of the party. On another occasion the frustration of Palestinians, faced with the loss of ancestral land to advancing settlements, evoked particular sympathy amongst co-religionist Muslim and Christian members of the party.

There was a suggestion that the disputed report might be withdrawn and efforts made to draw up a joint report with Jewish representatives for the following year. Those responsible indicated that they were very happy to consult with Jewish colleagues since dialogue and listening to one another's stories and perspectives was always important. However, they were equally clear that it was for the Church, after listening, to frame its own report. This view prevailed in the Assembly.

Luke thought how recently he and Joyce had entertained Ubayd and Misha and discussed joint projects. And now, he reflected, we're up against the reality that interfaith dialogue is not easy, at least not if we are really to engage in some depth with one another. Clearly the Assembly report did not make comfortable reading for the Jewish community. But was it impertinent for Christians to offer their own interpretations of Old Testament texts? After all, this was their Scripture too. The important thing, as the Assembly had been reminded, was to accept that sincerely held Christian and Jewish interpretations of the same texts might not coincide.

Shortly after the General Assembly Luke's attention was drawn to an article commenting on the controversy. In what he thought was a cogent paragraph the author argued that the real issue was not whether one or other community had a divine right to the land, but whether all the people living between the Jordan River and the Mediterranean Sea were treated with justice, equality, security and dignity under the law. This certainly struck a chord with Luke. Indeed, the very title of the article – *Can Christians advocate for Palestinian rights and not be anti-Semitic?* – seemed to go to the heart of the matter. This chimed with his own view that disagreement with aspects of Israeli government policy need not imply anti-Semitism or disrespect for the Jewish faith. Equally, he reflected, legitimate criticism of Palestinian policies should not be heard as a denigration of Islam or Christianity, the predominant faiths within the Palestinian community. That said, Luke also recognised, and strongly believed the Church should recognise, the appalling persecution of the Jewish people down the centuries, often at the hands of Christians. Memories were rightly long and the need for historical awareness and sensitivity in Christian-Jewish dialogue was ever present.

As he thought about this Luke found himself reflecting on just how much Christianity owed to Judaism. The Hebrew Scriptures make up more than half of its Holy Book. One of the lynchpins of the Reformation in Scotland had been the translation of the psalms into metre and set to simple, singable tunes. For centuries it was customary for only the psalms to be used in reformed worship. A concession was made in the eighteenth century when metrical paraphrases of other portions of Scripture were allowed. Not until the late nineteenth century were hymns of mere human composition permitted in Scottish presbyterian worship, and even then the custom was that the service would begin with a psalm. And while he hadn't kept a record Luke reckoned that the twenty-third psalm had been sung at half, if not more, of the funerals he had conducted over forty years of ministry. And to whom do we owe the psalms, he asked himself. Answer: the Jewish faith. To whom do we owe such rich texts as 'Comfort ye my people'; 'What doth the Lord require of thee but to do justice, to love mercy and to walk humbly with thy God?'; to whom do we owe the Ten Commandments and the wisdom of the Book of Proverbs? Again, the answer is the Jewish religion.

He recalled the phrase, 'People of the Book.' That's what we are, he mused – Jews, Christians, Muslims – People of the Book, children of Abraham, worshippers of the one God. Well, his musing continued, the first two statements are indisputably correct – but what about the last one? That's what Ubayd and I are supposed to be working on for the meeting in Capelaw in a few weeks' time.

But here's a thing, he thought. We <u>must</u> all believe in the same God because we all believe there is only one God. If that is true then either we all believe in that one God, or only one of us is right.

It's not so difficult, his musing continued, to think of Jews and Christians worshipping the same God. After all Christianity grew out of Judaism and, at the start, many people just thought it was another Jewish sect. When Christians read the Old Testament, for example the story of Moses being given the ten commandments at Mount Sinai, it's the same story that the Jews read in their Scripture, so we must be talking about the same God, mustn't we? A parting of the ways came a thousand and more years later with Jesus of Nazareth. There were Jews, like Saul of Tarsus, who accepted that Jesus was the promised Messiah. Meanwhile others rejected this belief, regarding Christianity as a heresy and adhering to the old faith and the long established traditions of their ancestors.

Then a few centuries later in the deserts of Arabia a prophet called Muhammad arose and attracted many followers. There had been revealed to him a new book called the *Qur'an* containing many passages which echoed both the Jewish and the Christian Scriptures. Like Christianity this new religion, which became known as Islam and drew on deep and ancient roots stretching back to Abraham, prospered and gained many followers. The term they used for God was *Allah* and the question then emerged how this *Allah* related to the God of the Jews and the Christians.

When the Syrian Mufti had talked about 'cousins in faith' he wasn't far off the mark. This thought prompted a memory of Luke's paternal grandmother who had been born and brought up in the Outer Hebrides. She had left her native island after school and had settled on the mainland of Scotland, marrying and bringing up her family in Glasgow. But Luke remembered being taken to Lewis as a child to visit what seemed to him very elderly relatives. His place within the 'clan' was always identified in relation to first, second, third and even fourth cousins. There was even someone who was referred to as a second cousin once removed. As a boy he thought that sounded quite exciting and wondered if perhaps the person had been executed.

Thinking back he recalled how, to him, all these cousins were strange and distant people. But somewhere, back in the mists of time, there was a common forebear. Why, only the other week he and Joyce had had Richard and family to stay and they had been showing grandchildren Katie and Marcus old family photographs. One very old black and white image showed Luke's mother as a little girl with her mother and grandmother. Joyce had explained to somewhat bemused children that these people in the strange clothes were their great, great-great and great-great-great grandmothers. As all three people in the photograph had had more than one child, Luke mused, there must be a positive tribe of cousins out there whom Katie and Marcus will never encounter, and would not recognise even if they did. 'Cousins in faith.' That's what the Mufti said. So it must be a bit like that for Christians, Jews and Muslims who together account for more than half the world's population. That's quite a thought.

What Luke and Ubayd were calling their 'public conversation' was scheduled for the late summer of 2013. The shocking murder of Drummer Lee Rigby on the streets of London in May had been a deeply disturbing event on many levels. It had stoked anti-Muslim sentiment with protest marches and attacks on mosques. In a phone conversation with Joyce Misha had mentioned a significant drop in numbers visiting their mosque, with many school children being withdrawn by their parents. Ubayd had also phoned Luke wondering whether they should consider abandoning, or at least postponing, their plan. He condemned the attack unequivocally but the last thing they wanted was to have their conversation in a hostile environment with potential for trouble. On the other hand, they both agreed, do such incidents not serve to underline the need for dialogue across cultural borders? This view prevailed and it was decided to continue planning for the meeting, but to be prepared to cancel should circumstances at the time suggest that would be prudent.

The subject of the 'conversation' had also come up when Richard and Alison had been visiting with the children. They had been invited to a wedding in Edinburgh and asked if they could stay for the weekend. It was going to be all too complicated to arrange baby sitters at home. Needless to say Joyce and Luke were delighted, but Luke would have to ensure that his Sunday preparation was complete before they arrived.

There wasn't much opportunity for grown-up conversation but Richard had asked how his father's interfaith involvement was going. He remained cautious, not so much because he thought it was wrong, but more out of concerns over possible antipathy – hostility even - towards his father.

"People feel pretty strongly," he had remarked, "particularly after the dreadful murder of that young soldier in Woolwich. If you go ahead you may have protestors turning up. You may start getting hate mail or worse – heaven forbid! We just don't want you getting hurt."

Luke had been rather thrown by this. Was he being idealistic to the point of naivety? It hadn't really occurred to him that a public conversation between a minister and an imam in quiet Capelaw could attract protestors. Should he let the police know about the event? Would local residents blame the church if anti-Muslim demonstrators turned up, disturbing the peace and perhaps damaging property?

What he didn't tell Richard (and had still to mention to Joyce) was that in the course of the past week he had received a couple of letters. The first of these was an anonymous and deeply unpleasant rant about the evils of immigration and how foreigners were taking over the country. The writer demanded to know why Luke wasn't upholding 'our Christian traditions' instead of undermining them? 'Like you are?' queried Luke. Over the years Luke had received the occasional anonymous letter and knew that the thing to do was immediately consign it to the wastepaper basket; but they were still unpleasant and unsettling and he had been brooding about it since it arrived.

The other letter was from a couple in his congregation, Ron and Betty Clark who, courteously but firmly, expressed their disagreement with the planned visit of the imam and announced their decision to move to another church. They had been uneasy about the Guild event last year but this now seemed a step too far. If people want to learn about Islam or any other religion they are free to do so, they argued but, as they put it, 'we don't need to have it served up to us on a plate in our own premises.' They went on to say that they had appreciated Luke's ministry and realised times were changing but, for them personally, it was time to move on. It was this letter, with its courteous regret, that caused Luke more distress. He knew the Clarks well and, only a couple of years ago he had officiated at the wedding of their daughter – a very happy occasion. Like many conservative Christians they had been loyal and supportive members and would be missed. He would make contact with them and offer to call round, but suspected their decision was final.

"It's not that I'm against it Dad," continued Richard, interrupting his father's brooding. "Really I'm not. But Anne and I have been talking on the phone. Of course she's over the moon about it and thinks it's a great idea. I'm just more cautious. But what we have agreed is that, if you do go ahead, we're going to come along. The date's in the diary and I'd be quite interested to see how it goes. But I do think you should let the local police know and perhaps also have another chat with your session clerk and some of the elders. You really must give some thought to security."

"You're probably right," said Luke, "though I don't know if you read that story the other day. A group of English Defence League members had turned up to demonstrate at a York Mosque and ended up sharing tea and biscuits with the Muslims. They even played football together. The Archbishop of York made some comment about tea, biscuits, and football being a typically Yorkshire way of disarming hostile and extremist views."

"Anyway," Luke continued, "the imam and I have had a conversation about the climate of opinion but are still minded to go ahead. I'm really thrilled, though, that you and Anne are planning to come. That will be hugely supportive. I'll have a word with Brian, the session clerk, next week and then perhaps he and I together can call in at the local police station. I'll also have a word with Bill Macrae. Do you remember Bill? He's quite senior in Lothian and Borders police and a member of the congregation. He'll be able to advise me."

"Now isn't it time you were getting dressed for this wedding?"

After the family had returned home and peace again reigned in the manse Luke followed up the various leads he and Richard had discussed. He shared the letters with Joyce who, like him, was sad about the Clarks and deeply irritated by the anonymous diatribe.

"I imagine that will make you even more determined to go ahead," was her response adding, before Luke could reply, "Quite right too. We can't let people who don't even have the courage to put their names to their opinions dictate what we do!"

Luke was simultaneously encouraged and relieved, even though he was pretty confident that his wife's reaction would be along these lines.

He also shared the letters with Brian MacFarlane, his session clerk, and mentioned the conversation with Richard. This served only to confirm anxieties which Brian was planning to raise with Luke. He didn't want to over react but had already decided to speak to Bill Macrae and take his advice. He was also of the view that as expectations had been created it really would be quite a big decision to abandon the plan. He was very reluctant to go down that road.

Luke was reassured by Brian's calm and confident approach. A few days later Brian got back to him to say that he had taken soundings and there was a clear mind to go ahead. He had also spoken to Bill Macrae who was following things up with a view to having a discreet police presence on the night.

"So we're all set," said Luke."

"Yes, replied Brian. "We're all set."

16

The day of the 'conversation' duly arrived. This was to be the first of two such gatherings, the second one being scheduled for the mosque two weeks later. There had been good feedback from the Guild event, nearly a year ago, and this had given a fair wind to the next step along the Capelaw road of Christian-Muslim contact. The determination not to cancel out of fear of possible protest was itself evidence of this positive feeling. Indications were that a good number of people planned to attend. Perhaps for some the motivation was simple curiosity – but that was all right, Luke thought. Curiosity is preferable to apathy.

There had been publicity in the church newsletter. In addition, the local newspaper had carried an advertisement as part of the usual church notice, along with a news item. This included a quote from the session clerk saying that the kirk session welcomed this interfaith initiative by the minister and the imam. He also stressed that anyone who wished to attend would be welcome.

In the event Luke's original hunch about numbers wasn't far off the mark. A mixed crowd of around a hundred people gathered in the church hall that evening. Around half were members of the congregation with the others drawn generally from the Capelaw community. Luke was pleased to see a number of senior pupils from the local secondary school and also spotted James Morrison, the presbytery clerk and his wife, Caroline, in the audience. The cautious Luke had again thought it prudent to keep James informed. As promised, Richard and Anne were there and Luke looked forward to a 'debrief' back at the manse afterwards. Richard was driving back to Fife so couldn't linger, but Anne was staying the night.

There was also a small demonstration outside the hall – perhaps a dozen people - with placards proclaiming Bible texts such as "Jesus said 'I am the way, the truth and the life; no one comes to the Father but by me'". It reminded Luke of the old days at the General Assembly when the late Pastor Jack Glass and members of his congregation would gather on the Mound outside the Hall to protest about the Kirk's ecumenical links, particularly with the Roman Catholic Church.

"The Clarks were quite right," whispered Luke to Joyce. "Times have changed. People now think we've moved beyond Rome to Mecca!"

"Well, we were right to be cautious," remarked Brian to Luke, surveying the scene and adding: "But at least it's not the 'Muslims go home' type of protest. That would be altogether more unpleasant. But we'd still better be prepared in case they try to disrupt the meeting."

At this point Bill Macrae arrived.

"Well, well, Luke, you're probably the first Capelaw minister to have pickets outside a church meeting. Knowing you you're probably quite chuffed," he added with a smile. "But I've tipped off the local team and they'll keep an eye on things and get a posse along here pretty quickly if there is any sign of trouble."

Luke stopped to speak to the protestors, as he had often stopped for a word with Jack Glass outside the Assembly

Hall. They were members of a small evangelical church in Edinburgh. The leader of the group, who was the church pastor, introduced himself as Peter Hendry and assured Luke that they were not there to cause trouble.

"We just want to make the point that what you are doing is so wrong. It's a betrayal of the Gospel. We are asserting our right to protest but will do so peacefully."

However, one member of the group was rather more aggressive. She wagged her finger at Luke:

"It's all very well for you folk out here with your smart houses and nice cars. Where I live in a housing scheme we've got asylum seekers and east Europeans. When I walk down the street I hear so many languages I sometimes wonder if I'm still living in Scotland. And then there are the gangs and the crimes. If you want to break down barriers, as you people put it, come to our church one Sunday and I'll show you round our community and you can meet as many Muslims as you want – Sikhs and Hindus too, for good measure."

"I'd be very happy to come over sometime," said Luke. "Your pastor knows how to get in touch with me."

At this point the pastor intervened:

"OK Mary, you've made your point. Let the minister get into his meeting."

"I may regret saying this," Luke replied, "but if you want to come into the meeting you are, of course, very welcome, provided there's no disruption."

"That's decent of you, but there's a bus back to Edinburgh in half an hour so we'll be on our way. But, seriously, think about coming over to see us. Here's my card. We don't all think like Mary. In fact we give a lot of support to asylum seekers, which doesn't win us Brownie points with everyone.

We also run a food and clothing bank and work closely with Fresh Start, the charity which recycles second hand furniture. We believe this is our Christian witness and we help people of all faiths and none. We just don't believe in compromising our own faith which is what I think you are doing."

"Well, your thinking is kind of obvious," replied Luke. "Maybe we should talk further, but not now. I'll think about coming over sometime."

Meantime, inside the hall, Misha had come with Ubayd and she and Joyce had sat together in the front row. Luke thought this was a nice touch and was pleased that he could welcome the mosque couple and that the warmth which had developed between Misha and Joyce would be evident. Ubayd was also accompanied by half a dozen members of the mosque management committee. He joked about his 'bodyguard', saying that when he saw the 'reception committee' outside he was glad he had brought them.

The evening opened with a welcome from Luke. Ubayd had provided the names and roles of those who had come with him so they were able to be recognised and introduced individually. Each one received a warm round of applause. Then Luke outlined the format of the evening. He explained that he and Ubayd had met on a number of occasions and this evening's meeting had developed from their conversations. Their plan was to 'jump in at the deep end', as he put it and begin by talking about God. Luke would say something about the Christian understanding of God after which Ubayd would outline Muslim beliefs. The meeting would then be opened up for questions and comments to which they would respond. Joyce and Misha exchanged smiles as someone in the row behind whispered to their neighbour: "I thought they'd start with the easy stuff and work up!"

Luke began by rehearsing the tradition of Christians, Jews and Muslims being 'people of the book' and sharing a common ancestor in Abraham.

He continued: "This is what lies behind the phrase 'Abrahamic faiths.' We often use the phrase 'multi-cultural' to describe our society and there are followers of a variety of religions in Scotland - Buddhist, Hindu, Sikh, and Baha'i. But Jews, Muslims and Christians claim a shared inheritance."

He then went on to explain that he and Ubayd had considered inviting a rabbi to join them this evening but had decided just to take one step at a time. If this goes well, he had added, a three-way conversation might be the next stage

"Given this history," he continued, "a question which has been asked is whether Christians, Jews and Muslims worship the same God, but just understand God in different ways. The challenging thing about this, though, is that all three religions are monotheist. They believe there is only one God – so if all three faiths don't recognise the same God presumably only one of them can be the true religion."

He smiled as he offered this last thought and observed the smile spreading through the audience.

He then went on to acknowledge that what was particularly distinctive about the Christian view of God related to Jesus Christ. "For Jews," he said "Jesus was a radical teacher who founded a new religion; for Muslims he was a very great prophet ranking even higher than Moses and Elijah. But for Christians he is far more than that. We believe Jesus actually embodied God, or to use the technical term, incarnated God. Does this mean Christians recognise two gods? Well it's even more complicated than that. We read in the Bible that after Jesus' death and resurrection a presence named 'the Holy

Spirit' came and filled the confused disciples with power. Was this then a third god? We don't think so. Rather we think that both Jesus and the Holy Spirit are manifestations of God and this is what lies behind the doctrine of the Trinity – not three gods but three aspects of the one God."

"One way of trying to illustrate this," Luke suggested, "is to think of how we all have different aspects and relationships. A woman can be a wife, a mother, a daughter, a work colleague, a friend. These are all different characters and roles and are addressed by different names – 'Mummy', 'Darling', 'Margaret', 'Mrs Smith' - but despite these multiple identifiers the woman remains one person. This is how Christians think of God as Father, Son and Holy Spirit, all bound up in the same person."

Ubayd began by thanking Luke for the friendship which had grown up between them. He thought it was appropriate that that last illustration had used a female example because it was really thanks to the women of the mosque and the church that this relationship had started. He had heard from Misha about the Guild meeting last year and now here was the next step on what he hoped would become a journey of faith and discovery. People would be very welcome to visit the mosque and have a tour. He understood the mosque women were arranging to host a meeting with the Capelaw Guildswomen later in the year, and he was looking forward to having Luke and some of the church members for a second 'conversation' at the mosque in a couple of weeks' time.

He then went on to say that Luke had put his finger on the essential difference between a Christian and a Muslim understanding of God.

"For Muslims God, whom we call *Allah*, is essentially one," he explained.

He continued: "This isn't to say that different attributes of God aren't acknowledged. We speak of God as king, as judge and as mercy. In fact the *Qur'an* mentions no less than ninety-nine names for God, such as 'the loving one' and 'the merciful one'. But an important text in the *Qur'an* states clearly that '*Allah* is One, the Eternal, the Absolute. He does not beget nor is he begotten and there is none like Him.'"

He then stressed that Muslims acknowledged and revered Jesus as a great prophet and that Jesus and his mother Mary are referred to in the *Qur'an*.

"However," he insisted, "Muslims cannot accept the claim that Jesus was divine."

When it came to questions someone asked Ubayd if he could explain the 'Five Pillars of Islam'. It was a phrase the questioner had often heard but he would welcome having it spelt out.

Ubayd duly obliged listing them one by one:

- There is no god but God and Muhammad is the Messenger of God
- Observance of regular prayer
- Giving alms (*zakah*) – Muslims have a defined obligation (unless really poor) to give 2.5% of savings per year to assist those in need in their community
- Fasting during *Ramadan* by avoiding food and drink between the hours of sunrise and sunset – exemptions apply for the sick and the frail
- The *hajj* or once in a lifetime pilgrimage to Mecca

Luke commented that, while not so formally listed, similar disciplines have formed part of Christian tradition. Lent is recognised as a season of fasting; there is an expectation that Christians will give 'as the Lord prospers them' and prayer, both within worship and private devotion, is fundamental to the Christian life. As for pilgrimages, these were very popular in the Middle Ages, but still today Christians will travel to places like Iona, Santiago de Compostela and the Holy Land.

Following on from this session clerk Brian MacFarlane asked if Ubayd could say a word about Muslim festivals. While terms like *Ramadan* were familiar enough Christians weren't really sure of their significance. Ubayd said he was happy to respond.

Picking up on the reference to *Ramadan* he explained that this marked the ninth month of the Islamic calendar, the month in which the Prophet Muhammad received the *Qur'an*. *Ramadan* was observed by fasting during the hours of daylight, a discipline designed to focus on the centrality of the *Qur'an* to all Muslims and of the Prophet to whom it was revealed.

"The month of *Ramadan*," he stressed, "is the most sacred in the Islamic calendar."

"*Ramadan*," he continued "is followed immediately by the festival of *Eid-al-Fitr* which marks the end of *Ramadan*. It is literally a feast to mark the breaking of the fast. Indeed it is forbidden to fast at *Eid*."

Ubayd went on to point out that *Eid-al-Fitr* is sometimes referred to as the lesser *Eid* distinguishing it from another festival called *Eid-al-Adha*. Referred to as the greater *Eid* this commemorates Abraham's preparedness to sacrifice his first-born son Ishmael in submission to God's command and his son's acceptance to be sacrificed, before God intervened to provide a lamb for sacrifice instead.

"Did you say Ishmael?" asked Luke. "Don't you mean Isaac?"

"Yes I did say Ishmael and No, I didn't mean Isaac," replied Ubayd with a smile. The story is the same as in the biblical Book of Genesis but in our version it was Ishmael, not Isaac who was about to be sacrificed."

"How interesting," said Luke. "You learn something new every day!"

"Another festival with links to a Bible story is *Ashura*," Ubayd continued.

He went on to explain that in *Shii* tradition this commemorated the martyrdom of the Prophet's grandson, while for *Sunnis* it recalled the crossing of the Red Sea by Moses and the Israelites. This latter focus derived from a tradition that when Muhammad arrived in Medina the Jews were observing a fast to mark their deliverance from Egypt.

Further questions followed. Most of these were directed towards Ubayd and related to issues such as the difference between *Sunni* and *Shia*, why men and women don't worship together and why Muslims don't drink alcohol or eat pork. There were some more 'edgy' questions, for example, asking what *jihad* means. Someone followed this up, rather aggressively Luke felt, with a question about extremist fundamentalism and its devastating effect around the world.

Ubayd responded by arguing that, just as there was a spectrum within Christianity so Islam had its extremists. How many people had lost their lives in the Inquisition, he wondered and from his limited knowledge of Church history he was aware that inter-denominational violence was all too common. But speaking for himself and those associated with his own mosque he had no hesitation in condemning terrorist atrocities. He also pointed out that many Muslims, just wanting to get on with their lives, were victims of extremist policies and violence. The Taliban attitude towards women's education was a case in point, recently highlighted by the case of the teenage Pakistani girl who had been shot in the head for standing up for the right to go to school. Fortunately she was making a good recovery, thanks to specialist medical care in England and was refusing to be intimidated. The great majority of Muslims, like the majority of Christians just wanted to live in peace, he insisted.

As the questions continued Ubayd whispered to Luke that people seemed more interested in these matters than talking about God.

"I think I could have predicted that," Luke whispered back.

Eventually there were no more questions and the meeting drew to a close. Session clerk, Brian MacFarlane proposed a vote of thanks and the applause was generous. Refreshments were then made available for those who wished to linger, mingle and converse.

The evening was a great success. This was Anne's unqualified view as she and her parents relaxed back at the manse. Luke and Joyce agreed that it had gone better than might have been expected. Luke had been particularly taken by a number of people saying how much they had appreciated the opening statements about God. These included people who weren't church goers and one of them had asked if he could come and see him sometime as he would like to reconnect with the church.

"I gave him my card,"Luke added. "I may hear nothing more, but you never know."

"And talking of cards," he continued. "Here's one I was given earlier."

He produced Pastor Peter Hendry's card and asked, "What do you think? Should I get in touch? Perhaps we could both go over," he said, looking at Joyce.

Their conversation was interrupted by the phone. Luke took the call and returned smiling.

"That was James Morrison – the presbytery clerk. He just wanted to say how much he and Caroline had enjoyed the evening and to say, 'well done.'"

"Good old James," laughed Joyce. I thought he'd be there. He really likes to keep his finger on the pulse and clearly, Luke, you are where the pulse is."

"Nicely put, Mum," added Anne. "Yes, well done, Dad. We're proud of you!"

Two weeks later Luke and Joyce, along with Brian MacFarlane, Neil Jeffrey, who had spoken so positively at the session meeting, Maggie, Jean and Moira went to the mosque for the second 'conversation'. Again there was a gathering of around a hundred, both men, women and, as at Capelaw, a good number of younger people. The format was similar to the Capelaw meeting, except this time Ubayd spoke first and then Luke. As at Capelaw the thrust of the questions related more to practical matters. Someone wanted to know about women ministers, when Jesus' disciples were all male. Luke explained that while the 'twelve' were male it was clear from the Bible that women were also his followers and some of them played an important role in the early church. Someone else asked Luke to explain the difference between Catholic and Protestant.

"How long have you got?" Luke replied, to laughter.

As at Capelaw a question about festivals came up giving Luke the opportunity to talk briefly about Christmas, Easter and Pentecost. There were also what Luke described as 'balancing' questions to those asked at Capelaw about terrorism and fundamentalism. These related to the often interventionist role of the 'Christian West' in the mainly Muslim Middle East. In reply Luke pointed out that Christianity too had originated in the Middle East but many Christians were now feeling unsafe and leaving the area. He also reminded the audience that many western churches had strongly opposed the invasion of Iraq.

"What now?"

This was the question Luke and Ubayd pondered when they met to take stock a few weeks later. Both agreed that the 'conversations' had been valuable occasions and that the reaction at both church and mosque had been good. The question now was how to build on what had been achieved.

"Well," said Luke, "perhaps we anticipated the answer in the two conversations we've just had. Did we not note that Christians, Muslims and Jews are the 'people of the book'? Do you remember David Amos, one of the rabbis on the interfaith pilgrimage? He invited me to his synagogue after we got back and we shared a question and answer session about the experience. We haven't really kept in touch but he's still in Edinburgh as far as I know. Why don't I get in touch and perhaps the three of us could meet up and take it from there."

"I'd be happy with that," replied Ubayd, "though the Israel-Palestine dimension brings added sensitivities to the table. And aren't your lot rather out of favour there after that General Assembly report?"

"Yes, that was a bit difficult," agreed Luke, "but is that not the point? There's little purpose in talking if we've nothing to talk about. Is interfaith not about tackling the hard questions and trying to set our disagreements within the context of a wider humanity and friendship?"

"That's certainly the ideal," agreed Ubayd. "So, yes, please contact David and let's take it from there."

That evening Luke told Joyce what he and Ubayd were now planning. She remembered David from the pilgrimage and thought it would be good to have him on board, if he agreed. I'll send him an e-mail tomorrow," said Luke. "Phoning might rather put him on the spot."

Next morning the e-mail was duly sent and within an hour David had responded, by phone. He had heard on the grapevine about what Luke and Ubayd were doing and would be more than happy to meet with them. "After all," he had added mischievously, "we are the senior Abrahamic faith!"

And so it was agreed that minister, imam and rabbi should meet together soon.

Meantime, Luke had a 'day job' at Capelaw Parish Church to be getting on with, though not for much longer. Retirement beckoned in just over a year. Plans would need to be made, not least as to where he and Joyce would live once they left the manse.

The Church of Scotland would proceed with its review of interfaith policy. Luke would have no formal role in that but his hope was that the sort of things he and like-minded colleagues had been doing would ensure a positive outcome, with a continuing commitment to dialogue, respect and friendship. Retirement would bring changes but the journey of interfaith discovery which had brought him so much enrichment would surely continue.

Lightning Source UK Ltd.
Milton Keynes UK
UKOW03f0917050514

231099UK00001B/10/P